As Good as Goodbyes Get

A Window into Death and Dying

BY JOY NUGENT

BALBOA.PRESS

A DIVISION OF HAY HOUSE

Balboa Press books may be ordered through booksellers or by contacting:

Balboa Press
A Division of Hay House
1663 Liberty Drive
Bloomington, IN 47403
www.balboapress.com.au
AU TFN: 1 800 844 925 (Toll Free inside Australia)
AU Local: 0283 107 086 (+61 2 8310 7086 from outside Australia)

Because of the dynamic nature of the Internet, any web addresses or links contained in this book may have changed since publication and may no longer be valid. The views expressed in this work are solely those of the author and do not necessarily reflect the views of the publisher, and the publisher hereby disclaims any responsibility for them.

The author of this book does not dispense medical advice or prescribe the use of any technique as a form of treatment for physical, emotional, or medical problems without the advice of a physician, either directly or indirectly. The intent of the author is only to offer information of a general nature to help you in your quest for emotional and spiritual well-being. In the event you use any of the information in this book for yourself, which is your constitutional right, the author and the publisher assume no responsibility for your actions.

Frank Stillitano MDIA
Creative Director
frank@designbyflux.com.au

Print information available on the last page.

ISBN: 978-1-5043-2343-7 (hc)
ISBN: 978-1-5043-0613-3 (sc)
ISBN: 978-1-5043-0614-0 (e)

Balboa Press rev. date: 11/12/2020

CONTENTS

ACKNOWLEDGEMENTS

My passion for nursing was nurtured by my Royal Brisbane Hospital tutor sisters, Joan Godfrey and Bartz Schultz, who have themselves been nurse leaders in the Royal College of Nursing Australia. It is with profound respect that I wish to acknowledge the support and encouragement given to me by my editor, Fiona Johnston. I very much appreciated the teaching received from Emeritus Professor Ian Maddocks AM and the patients and their families who invited me to share an important time in their life. I am proud of my four children and twelve grandchildren who have inspired me to live a life in which the soul has been the dominant guiding light. I acknowledge the influence and insights into Eastern thought gained by my travels to East and West Malaysia and remember fondly the strong friendships made from my association with the Sandakan Hospice in East Malaysia. Other mentors are acknowledged on my website: www.joynugent.com

FOREWORD

It was the spring of 1989 when my husband, David, was told by his surgeon to "go fishing." Having been diagnosed with bowel cancer in 1986 and having spent three years with ongoing surgery and various treatments, we now had to prepare for the next phase of our time together.

We had a property in the mid-north of South Australia, where we cropped and ran sheep and cattle. Our daughters, Sally, Mary-Jane, and Sarah, helped on the property during the holidays and *exeats*, or time off, from boarding school. David's surgeon referred us to Joy Nugent, private palliative care services, to assist us in the best way to move forward with comfort and confidence. We were quite taken aback with Joy's words, "Aren't you lucky to have cancer?" As time elapsed, it became clear what she meant.

We had time to plan what we needed to do to prepare for the amount of precious time we had together as a family. It was not possible for David to receive the care he needed and tend to our beloved property. We leased a town house and Joy and her team arrived to assist us through this time. Recovery from cancer was not an option for David, but removing fear and fostering realistic hope were options. Throughout this time David organized the sale of our property and farm equipment.

David's decision not to seek further active treatment was taken after a rather uncomfortable night when urinary function ceased. The peaceful atmosphere of a bedroom overlooking Aldinga Beach helped David and me to switch from the fight to beat cancer to dying well. David's peacefulness and courage came from the support of his family and friends.

David's room was seldom empty; there always seemed to be happy, teasing, satisfying reminiscences from all the facets of his life. The home environment made this possible. A minister visited and thought he was at the wrong house, as he could hear laughter coming from within. David, myself, and the girls received communion together.

We were always encouraged to participate in the nursing care. I will always remember one of my brothers trying to hold his nose as well as the basin of water while Joy changed the drainage bag that collected the strong smelling discharge from David's abdominal fistula.

The time from deciding to refuse further interventions to death was a week. David's palliative care doctor visited our leased Adelaide home. In that week David had eighty visitors.

David's death seemed timely. He indicated that he was comfortable and did not wish to hasten his death. He appeared to be waiting for his last visitor, who was a young farm hand he had helped. In his last moments, I whispered in his ear that it was time to go to join his mother for the Sunday roast (she died fifteen years before David). His final words to me were, "Keep on smiling!"

All the family was present when David quietly stopped breathing. Everyone who could fit in the room joined hands and said the Lord's Prayer before David was prepared for the funeral director. Sarah, his youngest daughter, took off her friendship bracelet of many years to tie around David's wrist. David, aged forty-nine, died in character and by his example took away the fear of dying for all those who were privileged to be with him during his last week.

Joy's care did not stop with David's death. She was there to help us plan the funeral and to choose readings for each of his daughters to read at his funeral service. At the funeral, a close friend who was to sing "The Rose" arrived in shorts, which was so symbolic of David's preferred dress. "Joy to the world" is what Joy has become to our family and a strong bond remains until this day.

—Margaret Drew

ABOUT THE AUTHOR

Joy Nugent completed her four-year hospital-based training at the Royal Brisbane and Princess Alexandra Hospitals before nursing in Canada at St Joseph's Hospital in Toronto. She completed the hospital-based training of midwifery at the Simpson Memorial Maternity Hospital in Edinburgh, Scotland, before nursing for a private nursing agency in London. For 30 years she was a wife and a mother to four children as well as working in her husband's orthodontic practice. A 'midlife crisis' came at age 48 which led her to complete a refresher course at the Royal Adelaide Hospital and returned to nursing—her 'unfinished business.'

Over the following three decades of nursing people at the time of death Joy has found herself compelled to seek an answer to: "What comes next?" Removing fear at the time of death has been a priority for Joy - She believes there is life in some energetic form after death. Indeed, one elderly man she cared for, who had been a mechanic, on hearing Joy express this, replied in a hoarse voice: "There better be!"

When Joy first began her career as a private palliative care nurse in 1987 she was asked to care for an elderly woman suffering from cancer. This woman was welcoming her death although she knew that her family would be upset. She had given her life to the selfless deed of translating books into braille and raising another woman's children as her own. Joy stayed with her for several nights until another referral called her away. When the dying woman was told of Joy's last night with her she said: "It's alright Joy we have met many times before and we will meet again." Joy replied that Dr Elisabeth Kubler-Ross said that the wisest people on earth are those who are dying and know it. Her comment in a steady calm voice was: "I think she may be right."

From that time Joy has been searching to make sense of the big questions in life. Why am I here? Is there life after death? When energy leaves the body after death what happens to it? Her journeying has taken her to study Eastern and Western traditions and philosophies. In 2013 she showed a copy of the book *Proof of Heaven,* by an American neuroscientist Dr Eben Alexander, to a man who was coming to the end of his life. He surprised everyone by dying unexpectedly and peacefully a day later. This doctor's words, to Joy's mind, replaced fear with curiosity.

In Joy's early palliative care nurse practice in two Australian cities she spoke to many people who had lived through near death experiences and received communications from the unseen world. One woman told of her experience during an episode of asthma. She said that she was floating near the ceiling of the bedroom and saw her dressing gown behind the door as well as her own body on the bed. Joy says that it is not uncommon for a person who is near death to see forms that bring comfort. One daughter reported seeing her mother was looking at a blank wall, smiling and nodding as if she were seeing a vision she recognised. Another woman told her that she received a message from another reality following the death by accident of her 18-year-old son. It had been a shattering loss until she saw her son's dog swimming lengths of her swimming pool. The dog hated water and wouldn't go near the pool normally and yet here it was giving this mother a sign that her son was fine - and perhaps even doing lengths - in another dimension.

Following her refresher course, Joy worked part-time at the Mary Potter Hospice in North Adelaide for 18 months. She was so inspired by this work that she helped to found the Mary Potter Foundation. But she also started to develop her own distinctive approach to care, a process that entailed pushing boundaries and always questioning the status quo. Always asking can this be done better? For three decades Joy successfully pioneered a private nurse practice in home-based palliative care. This model of nursing is described in her book, *New Nursing*, published in 2009. This book is available on her website: www.joynugent.com.

Many inspiring teachers have come into Joy's life. Her greatest inspiration has been the philosophy of Florence Nightingale (1820-1910) which Joy discovered in 1994. At a Nurse Healers' conference in Canada Joy listened to Janet Macrae speak enthusiastically of her part in bringing to print Nightingale's previously unpublished *Suggestions for Thought*. In *Suggestions for Thought* Nightingale wrote that she believed our life purpose is to grow from imperfection to perfection – and that more than one lifetime is needed to achieve that. The notion of reincarnation is one that Joy has explored from many ancient wisdom traditions. Like Nightingale Joy prizes freedom of thought and sees it as a privilege for oneself and a quality to respect in others. She includes snapshots of Nightingale's beliefs in *New Nursing*.

In *New Nursing* Joy writes about person-centered care - care that goes beyond what can be seen and measured. Person-centered care strives to listen to the inner life and to explore the message of myth— those cross-cultural stories that use supernatural or imagined beings or animals to depict a heroic journey such as the search for the Holy Grail or for awareness of the God within. In some way these stories connect a person to his or her own story or heroic journey, and the need to connect with the feelings, insights, and lessons that contribute to personal insight and growth.

For any one person there may be an important symbolic connection with the sea and its changing activity; the setting and rising sun; mountains with their call to conquer and stand firm; public figures or sports heroes; or with photographs, ornaments, clothes or possessions representing former or current roles. It is Joy's belief that rituals and symbols speak louder than words.

New nursing appreciates complementary therapies such as music and art therapy, massage and therapeutic touch, meditation, and guided visualisations. Being calm and living in the present moment or "now" is essential for nurses who wish to connect with the patient and their family in a soul-to-soul way, especially at the bedside of a dying patient. Joy writes that this intimacy remains long after the death of the patient and is the foundation for the grieving process, which is an important part of palliative care services. For Joy, the role of the nurse is to facilitate a healing process that honours the soul's journey and the choices made.

Being able to have deep conversations with patients and their families when they are searching for meaning or reflecting on the events of their life is a skill that has its roots in a nurse having the ability to search for answers to these questions in his or her own life. We all have a story and unresolved feelings. There are no right or wrong feelings; they may not be rational however they need appropriate expression. Many of the people in Joy's care suffered from dementia and she learned that acknowledging feelings rather than asking questions and seeking facts was often a more effective way of communicating.

Joy says there are times when the nurse is required to be a non-judgmental sounding board or bridge from one state of mind to another. This requires the skill of creative listening or a way of counseling which holds and turns the event, topic, or conversation like a cut diamond held up to the light. The person looking at the "diamond" may see the event, topic, or conversation in a new way, in a different light, and with more helpful insight. So it is with those who reflect on holistic care and what is required to facilitate the principles being taught and practiced widely.

Joy was the founder of NurseLink Foundation, which was a nonprofit public company with charitable status. She has a diploma in Clinical Hypnosis from the Australian Society of Hypnosis and seeks to continue to gain new insights into the mystery of life.

CHAPTER ONE

Introduction

Story has always been a means of learning lessons and, from fairy tales to the Bible, young and old have been able to absorb messages through the use of both the analytical left brain and the imaginative right brain. Palliative care has been called the science of the anecdote, and through sharing these stories I hope readers interested in palliative care, as well as the community at large, will benefit in whatever way is appropriate for them. Some may say after reading these stories that they would have acted differently in the past; some may see events in a new light. Whatever the reaction, I hope the stories will prove to be useful as we all struggle to make sense of our complex existence. The names and circumstances of the people involved have been changed as my intention is to protect those who may choose to see things differently through the lens of memory.

These stories represent my personal reflections and the lessons I have learned from them. They reveal my character and personal journey, for I believe we take ourselves, warts and all, to our work. We cannot give away what we do not have. Therefore, if I am full of doubts and fears, those are probably what I will project. Health professionals frequently project their personal fear of death onto those in their care, just as people with problems of unresolved grief frequently react to their projections.

MY FATHER'S DEATH

When I worked at Mary Potter Hospice in the early years of my palliative care work, I had the desire to assist the nuns with funds to buy more preventative equipment when it came to skin care. Years later, I realized during a course of hypnotherapy that I had not dealt with my own father's death some eighteen years earlier. When my father became a quadriplegic through suffering a spinal injury, I was expecting the birth of my first child, a son, in England, and I was not permitted to fly home. Before my father died a year later, he had developed a bad bedsore and I remember my mother writing to say that she was buying him a sheepskin for protection. I felt very frustrated at not being useful and supportive to my mother. Shortly after his death, my daughter was born in Rochester, New York, where my husband was a postgraduate student. On returning to Australia, I had two more children in a short space of time, and with four young children, and being in a new city, my time was filled for the next few years.

My grief and unresolved emotions surrounding the memory of my father were put on hold. Still on hold, they sought to surface with the image of a dying man with a bedsore at Mary Potter Hospice. Sometimes I think hospice workers are wounded healers struggling with their own insecurities and lack of sound belief systems. Certainly, many admit to the pain of some loss and how the direction of their lives turned to work in this area following an experience of loss and grief. So, for the stories and the insight I have gained into my own and others' emotions, I thank the many people who have been kind enough to share with me the intimacy surrounding an important life event.

MY EARLY NURSING YEARS

When I was a student nurse in the late 1950s, death was a mysterious and fearful event to be avoided at all cost. Dying patients were given frequent sips of water in the hope of keeping them alive until the next shift of nurses arrived. When death did occur, there was a dread on the part of the nurses of having to "lay the person out." This procedure involved a gown and a mask and a lot of cotton wool to pack orifices with the use of forceps. Strips of old linen were used to tie around the head to keep the jaw closed before the body was dispatched, via a wardsman and special trolley and as quickly and quietly as possible, to the hospital morgue. Death was somehow dirty and something that one didn't get too close to. A phone call was made to the relatives who were generally kept at arms' length and not encouraged to stay beside the dying person. They were not considered an integral part of the care as they now are since the modern hospice movement began in 1967 when Dame Cicely Saunders opened St. Christopher's Hospice in London.

After completing my nursing training at the Princess Alexandra Hospital in Brisbane, I travelled to Canada and worked in an orthopedic ward. I have no recollection of death ever occurring in what seemed to be an exciting new world. Following my Canadian experience I traveled to Edinburgh, Scotland, for midwifery training at the Simpson Memorial Maternity Hospital and experienced the joys and wonders of the birth of new life. The memory of the first birth I attended is still with me as I recall the proud young mother with her newly delivered baby talking to her husband on the bedside phone. I can now see similarities in the experience of a "good birth" and the experience of a "good death." Both are charged with emotion and signify a life change, which will not only entail long and sometimes arduous struggles but also bring rewards.

My career took me to London, where I worked as a private nurse and experienced death again. I was sent by a private nursing agency to nurse a fifty-year-old woman who was dying of breast cancer. This woman was being cared for at home by her only daughter who was in her mid-twenties, which was my age at the time. It was an experience now etched in my mind by its awfulness. I was instructed not to mention the word "cancer" and to express only hope for recovery and confidence in the doctor. Medications were not named or monitored; they were just given in blind faith because the doctor prescribed them. The tension of keeping up this pretense and not knowing what to say of comfort to the daughter and mother who were being parted was great. When the mother did die, the daughter was lost, as her mother had not been allowed to help her with practical instructions for a future without her. My heart went out to a girl of my own age and I accepted her invitation to stay in the apartment with her. Not knowing anything about a normal grief reaction, I seemed to get it all wrong. When I cleaned the walls of the bathroom, it was not appreciated and my actions were taken as a reflection on the inadequacy of the mother. My cooking was wrong; my company was sought but was resented. I left, but the memory stayed stored in me for many years until the death of my own mother at the age of seventy-nine when I was in my early forties.

MY MOTHER'S DEATH

Several weeks before my mother's last Christmas, I was walking by a dress shop when I suddenly thought of her and went into the shop to buy her a dress for Christmas. When I arrived home, she was still on my mind and I decided to place a long distance telephone call to her. No answer. I felt uneasy. I tried to phone my brother who lived in the same country town, but there was no answer. I phoned her doctor, who told me that he had her in hospital for investigations, as she was unable to swallow. I arranged for her to be transferred to a private hospital in another town where the investigations could be completed earlier by a surgeon I knew. Having organized care for my children, I traveled to be with her. What alerted me to her need? I was her only daughter and came along late in life after a stillbirth and two boys. I was much wanted and just a "joy." I was not given a second name.

I have always been an adventurous soul and left home for boarding school on my own request at the age of fourteen. After boarding school I lived in the nurses' home before my adventurous spirit took me overseas to further my nursing career and, as it turned out, to marry. My mother must have missed the daughter of her dreams but she accepted who I was and tried to support me. Looking back, I feel that I could have been more dutiful and attentive, although the boarding school habit of writing home a weekly letter stayed. Somehow, she was prepared to pay the price for my freedom. Now, following surgery, she was diagnosed with secondaries in the liver and an unknown primary tumor. The surgeon broke the bad news gently as he held her hand and told her he was not able to fix the problem. The private hospital staff members were accepting of the fact that their patient's daughter was a nurse who wished to be involved with her mother's care. "My daughter will shower me," my mother told the nurses when I went to the hospital to take her home in the dress I had bought as a Christmas present.

We both knew that time was limited. My previous experiences of death were no preparation, so I trusted intuition and was strengthened by my mother's faith in me. My mother had fought all her life for a balance between active involvement in church and community and depression. As a small child I felt that I had two mothers and often wished with a heavy heart that the good fairies would take my sad mother away and bring back the one who played me to sleep with "Over the Waves" on the organ. Music and painting were a large part of my mother's life. She played the organ for the Methodist community and was proud that one of her paintings had won a prize at the Brisbane Exhibition. When she came home from hospital, she chose to sleep in the front room of her small cream brick house which had, some years before, been purposely built so that my father could live there when he came home from hospital as a quadriplegic after a spinal hemorrhage at the age of sixty-six. My father died in the local town hospital before coming home for his final days could be a reality.

The front room had been kept for visitors but now it was where my mother chose to end her days. Her garden was her pride and joy and she knew all the botanical names of the plants in her care. The day we arrived home and wheeled up the ramp prepared for my father's wheelchair, her gardener came and she could hear the reassuring sound of the lawn mower. I picked flowers from her garden and placed them in her room. The atmosphere was good as neighbors called and well-wishers phoned to receive the news that jaundice was setting in and it was just a matter of time. The local doctor did house visits and was supportive of my wish to keep her at home—at least until she became unconscious. The minister visited and read her familiar Bible passages. Perhaps her biggest comfort was her little tape recorder and the Scottish tapes of empowering songs and hymns which she played, especially in the early hours of the morning when she felt most vulnerable to negative thoughts. One night she dropped her bundle and was bemoaning her worthlessness, and I begged her to stay strong so that I would have happy memories of our last days. She said that she was trying. Now I say to parents who are dying that they are about to give their children a most precious gift: the gift of example and courage. Stories are told about the need for children to release their parents and "letting go" is encouraged. "I'll see you tomorrow, Mum," may mean that Mum will be there because that is what will please her daughter. "Mum, I know that you are having a struggle and although I love you and will miss you, please let go if you are ready," may be an example of how to "let go" is also to love.

My mother and I only had a week together, but each moment was special as I sorted through her belongings, knowing that the time I could spend away from my four children was limited. She told me who was to have her paintings, her dinner set, the electronic organ she took to old folks' homes for sing-alongs, and her clothes. The nursing homes she visited were for other people and, although she was nearly eighty, she had never thought of herself being in one. While sorting through her desk, I came across a letter to Santa Claus that my brother had written and I found letters of utter despair written when my mother lost connection with her God. I filled many garbage bags with what I thought was rubbish and put aside the special requests. I now know that haste in these matters is not a good idea, and I regret so much, having thrown out the sheet music that she had kept from her youth, including my favorite, "Over the Waves."

One brother chided me for having thrown out rags, which would have been useful for cleaning his trucks. It was a time of high emotion when rational decisions were not made. My childhood memories, good and bad, were flooding over me. My relationship with my elderly parents, my father's death—which I discovered later was a matter of unresolved grief— my rebellion against the religion of my parents, and the relationships within my own family were all issues that were surfacing. Through all this were the demands of hosting the visitors, nursing my mother, involving my two brothers in the decision making, providing food, and being concerned with the activities of my own family. I was getting little sleep and hired a night nurse so I could spend a day with my family, who had arrived at the local seaside for a holiday. Before I left, I had my mother's medications and opioid injections organized and documented. I knew nothing in those days about hospice or the principles of palliative care, but I knew I didn't want my mother to suffer. She was worried about her bowels, which to her mind, had to open daily. Even they were organized before I left with the reassurance that I would return in twenty-four hours. When I did, I was greeted by a most unhappy mother, who asked me why I had taken so long. The night nurse had not kept up her regular injections because in her opinion it was too early. "Too early" were words that would ring in my ears years later when I heard the same fear of pain relieving medication being expressed. How can it be too early to be comfortable when one has a terminal illness? How can it be too early for the relief of physical discomforts, which hopefully will make way for retaining control of the mind?

From that moment my mother's condition deteriorated. I could scarcely move her feet to get her back to bed from the commode chair. The district nurses came to help, putting my mother on an alternating pressure mattress and inserting a catheter to avoid the strain and stress of going to the toilet. The doctor asked if I wanted her moved to hospital. In my mother's mind, nursing homes and hospitals were places to visit other people, and I remembered the many months of hospital visits she had made to my father. I felt there was no way I could move her from the security of her own bed, in her own home, and all that was not only familiar to her but *her*. I could not abandon her to the care of strangers. I wanted no more bad experiences with hired nurses. She was my mother and I was determined to see it through.

My eldest brother came to support me and we were both with her when her breathing stopped. The district nurses had just been there to wash her and sit her up on her pillows. A few minutes after the realization that my mother had died sank in, the nurses appeared again. Something had told them to come back because I needed them.

A neighbor appeared and took my brother and me for a cup of tea while the nurses contacted the funeral directors. When I returned, the bed was empty and the bedspread was neatly replaced on the bed. It was as if the event of a few hours earlier had been erased and now numbness set in. Like a robot, I made phone calls and looked forward to a lot of rest and the comfort of my own family. I didn't know anything about grief reactions and it was years later when I began to learn about hospice care that a lot of what I experienced at this time made sense. What I did know was that I had somehow been there when I was needed, as if I had fulfilled a bargain that my mother and I had made when I was given my freedom all those years ago.

In hindsight I realize that survival then took over and the demands of a young family largely put my grief on hold. I took comfort from the number of people who came to the funeral service and from the letters and cards that I received and diligently answered. When my nephew bought the house he needed a shed. This meant that some of the garden had to go. I was sad when I thought of my mother's love and care for her garden. Now I understand the lesson of impermanence. The garden was a part of her life's work which was now ended. It was now time for another to leave an imprint of a different kind.

For many years, moments of sadness would randomly surface. They came on the golf course, they came when I received flowers, they came at my children's end of year school activities, and they came when I wanted to share something special. The feeling I had through all my adventures was that my mother was always there, just like a baby playing peek-a-boo, and that while other people cared for me, no one cared in the same way. A mother's death is tied up with our own sense of beginning and ending, our own sense of love and nurture, our own sense of sacrifice and lifetime commitment. I was a mother of four children and had a strong spirit of independence and survival, yet it was humbling, painful, and very valuable to play a part in supporting my mother at the time of her death. It wasn't at all like the deaths I had experienced as a student nurse, or like the death in London of that other mother who had a daughter my age. It was an honest occasion and I wished more people could have this intimate knowledge of death.

MY RETURN TO NURSING

It was to be some years before my restlessness relentlessly prodded me to return to nursing. I had not practiced my profession for twenty years and fortunately, through a shortage of nurses, the opportunity to complete a refresher course at a large teaching hospital came my way. It was difficult to step out of my routine of following my children's activities, working in my husband's orthodontic practice, playing bridge and golf, having dinner parties and exciting holidays, and to enter a world of regular working hours, two thousand word essays, and wearing the blue uniform of a refresher student. As well as catching up on how to write a nursing care plan and give a presentation, time was spent at the bedside.

Again, death confronted me in an unpleasant way when I was assisting another nurse in washing an elderly woman who had had a stroke. She was in a coma and I noticed her pulse was weak and rapid and that her breathing was irregular. Her husband came to visit and I encouraged him to sit by the bed and hold his wife's hand. I thought she was dying and I thought his presence was more important than our activities. Just as he was settling down, the team of doctors arrived for the usual ward round. One of the junior doctors looked across the patient to the husband and, on consulting the notes, began to talk about nursing home placement for his wife. I was surprised, but who was I to question? Surely he had observed the patient's condition?

The husband left and we continued to change the bed and finish the bed bath. Just as we were finishing, the patient gave a sigh and became very pale and still. She had left us. Where was her husband? With the talk of nursing home placement, he obviously felt that there wasn't any urgency for his presence. It was several hours before he could be contacted and by the time he parted the curtains around the bed, his wife was covered with a white sheet. No longer did nurses pack orifices or use linen to close the mouth, but her hospital number had been written with a felt-tipped pen on her leg and her straightened body had been placed in a plastic bag ready for removal. The husband was taken to a side room and given a bag containing his wife's possessions. What else transpired I do not know, but I was appalled by the whole episode and the conviction grew that I needed to be more assertive and trust my own judgment if, as a nurse, I was to bring about an atmosphere like the one which surrounded my mother's death.

MY GROWING AWARENESS OF PALLIATIVE CARE

Another case stays in my mind from my time as a refresher student. A woman, who was about sixty, had a gangrenous leg elevated on a pillow. Her cancer was responsible for the blockage of blood supply to her leg and other medical conditions prevented amputation of the painful limb. She was being kept alive with intravenous fluids and was given injections of small doses of morphine for pain. The nurse looking after her kept records of her pulse and blood pressure. I was told she had no immediate family and certainly she looked to be in a depressed, unhappy, and uncomfortable state. My heart went out to her, and on her request the pain relieving injections were increased. That is, until the nurse recording her blood pressure reported she was refusing to give the next injection because the previous one had lowered her blood pressure. The level of blood pressure was more important than the level of pain relief. I couldn't believe it and raised the matter at tea break. Later a social worker was sent to talk to me, for it had been reported that I was distressed about the case. It made no sense to me to prolong this woman's dying process with intravenous feeding and reduced pain-relieving medication. I cannot recall the end of the story, but I remember the strange priorities that the student nurse, who had studied medicine for a few years before changing to train as a nurse, projected when she refused to administer the due medication. It was more important, in her opinion, to allow suffering than to take responsibility for a pain-free transition from this life to the next. Hiding behind hospital procedures masked the fear of death and a distancing from death, and insistence on such things as four hourly observations replaced a genuine concern for the real needs of this patient.

Thankfully, in the more enlightened ways of the hospice movement, tests and observations are not done unless the results can, in some way, add to the patient's comfort. Yet even here there is a paradox. Taking the patient's pulse is something I often do but seldom record. It is one of the most reliable indications of approaching death as well as being a time honored valuable connection between patient and doctor or nurse. I have often been critical of doctors when a dying patient is disturbed with the use of a stethoscope, but maybe this is a symbolic connection and a comfort to the family, too. I feel the importance lies in the intention. A calm, loving, inactive presence may be appropriate in some cases and loving, concerned, but fruitless actions appropriate in other cases. Sometimes traditional observations are understood by family and friends to be an expression of care and concern. Health professionals may be lost for "right" actions and responses because they lack palliative care training. I am learning that right or wrong ways and actions are not the issue but that the intention behind the action is the key. To take no action is often the harder, but more appropriate, decision. It needs to be remembered, however, that like parents, health professionals can only act with the knowledge they have at the time.

A dilemma arises when a doctor is faced with the decision whether or not to withdraw treatment. Often the decision to continue treatment gives the patient and his or her family time to adjust and the ethical principle of "doing no harm" might well be applied. At this point, considerations for the larger picture of community versus individual begin to surface. Can the community afford to give costly health care to a dying person for what may be only psychological reasons and impoverish other aspects of the health care budget? Who decides? Who pays? Will continuing to give food and fluids only add to the patient's burdens and indignities?

I recall a very elderly patient in the hospital where I completed my refresher course. This patient knew she was dying, but what troubled her most was the fear of incontinence. She didn't want to drink because she didn't want to have an "accident" in the bed. Dehydration, however, was not an acceptable option for the diligent professional staff and intravenous hydration was commenced. The result was that the woman died a week later in a wet bed. Instead of intravenous hydration, why wasn't her mouth just kept moist and clean? Why wasn't a catheter considered? Surely it was worth the risk of infection to preserve this lady's dignity. These issues arise frequently and, without thinking, health professionals may react as they would in life saving circumstances. To distinguish the subtle change from a life encouraging situation to a death-accepting situation is difficult for health professionals and lay people alike. Another layer of difficulty is added when what the patient mouths consciously is often not what is going on at a deeper level of awareness. "Please listen to what I am not saying" is the underlying plea to which the listener must respond.

MARY POTTER HOSPICE

From my refresher training, I went to work at a hospice run by an order of Catholic nuns. The founder of The Little Company of Mary was an English woman named Mary Potter. From small beginnings at the turn of the twentieth century, this woman had succeeded in her determination to bring about loving care for the dying and hospices were started up in several parts of the world. On my first visit to the Mary Potter Hospice in Adelaide, I was taken aback and rather bewildered when one of the nuns asked me if I would like to see one of their patients who had just died. Not wishing to be impolite, I followed her into a room lit with the glow of a candle at the bedside. In the bed, which was covered with a magnificent lace bedspread, was the still body of a middle-aged woman. Her hair had been brushed and arranged naturally on a pillowcase, which matched the bedspread. Her hands, which were placed on top of the bedspread, clasped a rose and rosary beads. She looked so beautiful and I kept looking for the rise and fall of her abdomen. I was starting to appreciate the different attitude toward death in this hospice compared to death in the large impersonal teaching hospital I had just left. The nun explained that the relatives were coming back to spend time with the person who had just died and together we placed chairs around the bed for this special time. Preparing the body after death was a ritual to be honored at this hospice. The beautiful linen was a part of the ritual. The lighted candles were replaced in time with a small electric flame in consideration of setting off a false fire alarm, but the stillness of the little hospice chapel and the prayers in the corridor before work each morning helped to maintain a feeling of peace and purpose.

Just as I remember significant patients from my refresher course, I remember significant patients from my time in the hospice. The first was a man from a foreign country who was dying of cancer that had spread to his bones. He was proud of his independence and strength as he told me of his struggles to make a living for his family as a tailor. Not long after coming to Australia he was involved in a car accident, which left him with the back injury that was now aggravated with cancer secondaries. The staff in the hospice, as if keen to compensate for other people's frequently inadequate giving of medication, insisted that he have morphine for his pain. He resisted, to their bewilderment. When I was sponging him and providing an inquisitive mind, I was amazed to hear him thank me for honoring and supporting his wishes not to have medication. He said that pain reminded him of love and that he was moving out of the valley of life so he could appreciate the beauty of the valley of life. Surely that is what is meant by transcendence? Being able to rise above a feeling or situation and see and experience beyond. I wished I could have had more time with this wise man for this little sip of insight must have come from a deeper well. However, I had been brought up to belief that religion, politics, and sex were not subjects to be discussed. Thirty years later I attended a meeting of people interested in spirituality. At the meeting the presenter distributed a book of collated talks this man had given to a Spiritualist Church. Heaven works in mysterious ways!

It was difficult for me to find the words in another Mary Potter Hospice situation when a man looked me in the eye and asked if he was dying. All I could do was kiss his forehead and feel sadly inadequate. Yet when I did eventually find the courage to talk to these patients about their funerals, have a final game of bridge, and facilitate toasts to their life, I was looked at sideways by fellow staff. I was beginning to step outside the bounds of what was then considered proper conduct for a hospice. The unspoken question on everyone's lips was the existence of life after death. Here were people about to set out on the great final journey and there was a conspiracy of "we know best and ask no questions." Whose needs were we meeting? Probably our needs, because hospice workers have a reputation for wanting to be in control, and it was threatening for us not to have the answers.

I developed a rather glib response to the question of life after death, saying I didn't need a carrot in this life to be good and if there was life after death it was a bonus. I cringe when I think of the shallowness of this reply, but at least it may have given the patient and family the message that I wouldn't entirely avoid the question, and hopefully an opening was made for further questioning. I remember being summoned before the head nun because a minister had complained I had embarrassed him in front of a patient with such a comment. It seemed that to step outside the words of God as written in the Bible was indeed dangerous territory. But what were we to say to patients and their families who did not find comfort in the words and rituals that were foreign to them or caused distress due to hidden resentments, fears, and guilt? The hospice philosophy encompasses the physical, intellectual, emotional, and spiritual needs of the patient and ideally integrates those needs into an holistic health picture.

TOWARD HOLISTIC PALLIATIVE CARE

Holistic health care—how can that be documented and incorporated into a care plan and be measured to satisfy those who measure quality by compliance? One of the first things I did when I left the Mary Potter Hospice was to attend a residential workshop, "Life, Death, and Transition" with Elisabeth Kubler-Ross. This was a steep learning curve for me, as I had never before been exposed to so much personal pain as we, as a group, listened to the stories of those present long into the night. Elisabeth Kubler-Ross teaches that emotions need to be released for healing to take place and likens the process to the release of pus from a pimple. Emotions such as resentment, hurt, envy, anger, guilt, and even love were expressed, and former hurts and behaviors, represented in pinecones and twigs, were symbolically thrown into an open fire before the time-honored symbols of bread and wine were shared. Contemporary mystic Caroline Myss stresses the need for a form of confession and ritual.

This workshop was the first time that I had met a person suffering from AIDS or a person who was HIV positive. One of the course participants was a man in his twenties who told me that he was expected to die in six months' time. He said he had chosen to stay in Australia because his parents in America had disowned him and the health supports in Australia were accessible. His mother had cancer and he was concerned for her and was feeling the burden of so many feelings and concerns. At that time many hospices were fearful of the reactions of their staff and other patients if they were to admit a patient with AIDS. At the workshop we were all one and at the end of the week many of our previously held attitudes had changed, and I personally felt that my life would never be the same again.

During the teaching sessions at the workshop, I learned a person could be represented by a circle divided into four quadrants to represent physical, intellectual, emotional, and spiritual needs. Each quadrant needs equal attention if a balanced life is to be achieved. This is the model I have used as I have attempted to invite expression of the needs of those whose lives I have been privileged to share. So often words stay just words and I feel "holistic" is one such word that needs visual expression to reveal its true meaning. I expand this concept further in my book, *New Nursing*.

THE SEARCH FOR MEANING AT THE END OF LIFE

Much is said about the search for meaning at the end of a life, and it was an elderly, popular Irishman at the Mary Potter Hospice who gave me a lasting example of this. One evening as I was attending to a patient opposite him, I observed that his breathing had changed and I went over to his side. I was feeling his pulse as I looked across the bed to where his wife sat holding his hand. I asked her how she was and she replied that her two sons were looking after her well. One had brought her to visit and the other was named positively. As she praised the two men, I stroked the man's brow and said, "You've done well, haven't you?" It was so uncanny, for at that moment, as if his mission was complete, he died. It is hard to describe the feelings of peace and love held in that moment.

I had learned another lesson from a man who was dying at home. His wife was caring him for most diligently, and when I first met him he expressed his appreciation of being at home and said he had too many memories of hospital visits and procedures for his liking. His shortness of breath required continuous oxygen and his wife had been dressing the fistula in his abdomen with a pad intended for menstruation. He laughed about that. There were many twists and turns in the efforts of those attending to his daily needs to make him comfortable. One day I was helping another nurse with his bed bath, and while he was on his side with his face to the other nurse he asked her if he was dying. It was a sudden question and the nurse responded immediately with a kindly, "Yes." He was rolled back toward me and I repeated the positives I had heard from his wife in a clumsy attempt to make him feel good. He looked at me and said, "It is all right, Joy. I got the message." When he had drifted into a coma and good-byes had been said, it was his wife who suggested that the oxygen tubing be removed from his nose. This was another lesson for me. I was used to using oxygen to promote a sense of doing something and to relieve feelings of helplessness. I was a little fearful of suddenly ending this life by its withdrawal, but I need not have worried, for it appeared to make no difference in the slow process of the breath's cessation. What was more important was the fact that the wife was letting go and the last image she had of her husband alive was not marred by technology.

ATTENDING TO LEGAL NEEDS

Another patient at Mary Potter Hospice who stays in my mind was a middle-aged man with a head of thick curly hair and a thick curly beard. His only visitor was his sister, who sat quietly at the end of his bed. It was the weekend and I had time to fulfill this man's request for a haircut. I sat the man out of bed and placed a draw sheet around his shoulders and proceeded to trim both hair and beard. Intuition has been the source of a large part of my words and deeds in my nursing practice —right or wrong. This time it was right, for when I said intuitively that having got his physical appearance in order, maybe it was time to attend to his legal needs, his sister opened her handbag and produced a will document, which she had purchased at the newsagent. She had wanted to bring up the matter but was fearful of creating the wrong impression and I had now given her the opportunity.

I place legal issues such as the making of a will, appointing an enduring power of attorney, and making an advance care directive in the quadrant of intellectual needs, for they are matters requiring much thought and some hard decisions. In the case described above, the need to talk about such matters was facilitated by a nurse going about her routine care. The nurse has a very special place in patient care, being involved in the intimate care of the body minus the clothes. The information gained either through the senses or through intuition forms the basis of the patient/nurse relationship. Many times it is the nurse who sees the patient experiencing pain on movement, vomiting while cleaning their teeth, or crying into their pillow. When the doctor asks a patient so neatly tucked up in bed how they are feeling, frequently the reply is, "I'm fine." Nurses therefore need to be aware and effective advocates for their patients.

REFLECTIONS ON PRIVATE PRACTICE

When I started a private palliative care practice in 1987, there was much criticism from those working in traditional hospice settings. But I would reply, "People won't pay for something that they don't value, so let the market place be my judge." There are also people who don't value something if they haven't paid for it. In the beginning of my practice I trained volunteers, but they were difficult to place in the private sector. It seemed that if one accepted the services of a volunteer, there was less control and gratitude was expected. If the "volunteer" was to be paid even a small amount, then the person requiring the services felt they could ask for what they required and also have some say in choosing their caregivers. Then there are the people who want everything for nothing and see it as their right to have everyone attending to their every whim. I have found that the people who tap into welfare are often the people not in need but rather they or their families have the know-how to obtain funds or services.

How to be fair and equitable? Is striving for fairness and equality a worthy goal, or would it be better to foster compassionate hearts and minds and honor some greater scheme of things? I see the genuinely needy as often missing out, for there are many who lack the confidence to ask for their needs to be met or know who to ask for help or are too proud to ask for help. I have experienced the most incredible generosity from relatively poor people and see many sides to the "god" of gold and silver. What is the meaning of karma or cause and effect or life giving us what we need rather than what we deserve? I still ponder on the events that have led me to some of the people I have cared for.

CHAPTER TWO

When is it Time to Die?

Maggie was in her sixties and had led a life that spanned three continents and many walks of life including theater and photography. She was divorced and those closest to her were her two daughters and her brother. When I met her, the daughters, who lived in England, were concerned to set up support networks for their glamorous mother who was suffering from a disease that required a continuous flow of oxygen to maintain any daily activity. Perhaps the first time we really got past the pleasantries and history taking was when I removed her soft blue leather slippers and massaged her feet. No wonder hairdressers are such effective counselors and dumping grounds for the concerns of those in the chair in front of them. It seems that making contact with a person via the head or feet is an indirect, non-threatening, acceptable approach when talking about subjects that are difficult.

During the foot massage we talked about life after death and I learned Maggie had often visited a medium and believed in a spiritual existence. Her direct approach to the other world bypassed traditional religious practice but it was nevertheless a comfort to her. For several months, other nurses, doctors, and I visited Maggie and helped her with washing, bed-making, and meals. More importantly, the company allayed some of her fears, for she was very fearful. She was fearful of the pain in her back, she was fearful of being alone, and she was fearful of the huge leap she was about to take. She admitted herself to hospital in one attack of panic, for as with so many people, hospitals are seen to be places where bodies could be patched up regardless of their state.

I suggested a wheelchair for walks around the block, but being seen in a wheelchair was not acceptable to this lady who cared so much about her appearance. She loved the luxuries of massage and being dried after a shower with towels pre-warmed in the tumble dryer. She enjoyed looking through photograph albums from the shelf of albums, which depicted the journey of her life. She organized her death notice and the address list of those she wished to be notified of her death. She took her tablets from the long line of medicine bottles and she received many visitors, yet she was restless.

Maggie's brother came to visit and helped to lift the burden for a time. He spoke to her doctors and helped with her legal affairs. Her younger daughter came to visit from England and, concerned for the aloneness of her mother, asked me to tell her mother that it would be a privilege if she were to give up the struggle for life while she was there. She said it would be a comfort to her if she knew her mother didn't die alone. Maggie was touched and for the first time I saw her cry. She thought it was a mother's duty to spare her daughter the pain of parting and here was her youngest daughter seeing that being able to share the parting was a special gift.

It never ceases to amaze me that the mind can be so powerful and play such an important part in the timing of death. Here was a woman who had gained her self-esteem from being in control and now she wanted to control her death. This was new territory for me and I felt that all I could do was watch, be supportive, and learn. Learn I did, for one night I was called to find my patient propped up in bed instructing her daughter about her funeral arrangements and the nightdress she would like Joy to put on her. She was breathless but excited and asked to be alone to settle for the night. Mary's daughter and I sat over cups of coffee and I became acquainted with her family through the photographs she had brought to show her mother. Later during the night, her daughter and I went to check on Maggie and found her breathing shallow. I took her limp arm to make a mental note of her pulse and found that it was scarcely discernible. What happened next will stay with me forever. Maggie lifted her arm and passed the back of her hand across her forehead and said clearly, "I'm fine." Her breath stopped completely within an hour. Maggie's spirit didn't seem to need her handicapped body any more. Maggie's other daughter arrived the next day and together the girls slept in their mother's bed. I used to joke with Maggie and tell her to come back and rattle our coffee cups at the funeral to let us know that she was all right. My coffee cup didn't rattle, but I felt that "I'm fine" was a sign indeed.

CHAPTER THREE

Different Ways of Dying

There is no pattern to the way people die, as character, beliefs, and readiness all play a part. For Maggie, it was time to go and her memory brings into my thoughts Mia, who was also a strong, controlling woman. Mia was 40 years old and stunningly beautiful. With a wig to cover her bald head from chemotherapy, few people would have recognized a woman with a short time to live. After having been diagnosed with breast cancer, Mia went on to breast feed the last of her four children, snow ski, model for fashion and photography, and indulge in her passion for catering, presenting the finest foods made with the utmost precision to the recipe. Conventional treatments were resorted to in an attempt to hold back the hands of the clock representing Mia's life. In spite of having had both breasts removed and courses of chemotherapy, secondaries were breaking through the skin on her chest and her abdomen was almost solid with tumors. But Mia, looking strikingly attractive with her bare head, took her children shopping and scolded them when their diets were not healthy and their manners were not impeccable.

Mia was weak and had been near death several times, but each time she found the strength to continue her life. Mia enjoyed the comfort of a special friend, who would lay beside her most nights reading poetry and together imagining a different world. Mia had a sexual energy that radiated in spite of her diseased body. She said her sexual desire was the first thing to return following her chemotherapy treatments. Mia had many loyal friends, male and female alike—even her doctors succumbed to the energy felt in holding her hand and looking into her eyes. The young lawyer handling her affairs was also touched by the strength of this woman and one day, just weeks before her death, I found them discussing her legal situation in the garden of the cottage. Mia was so alive, yet her body was an utter mess. She luxuriated in a warm bubble bath, she admired the floral arrangements that filled her little cottage, she listened to music, and she sat by an open log fire and meditated to the sounds of Tibetan bells. She had food to be "normal" with her children, all the while knowing that she would vomit later.

The cancer reduced her to skin and bone but still her spirit shone. At times she would talk about dying and make preparations. Most of the time, however, she would deny it was happening and she pressed on with alternative therapies and psychic healing. For me, my attempt to meet her needs was always like treading on eggshells without wanting to break them. She would call me in the early hours of the morning and I would find her wanting to die as she vomited copious amounts of foul fecal-smelling fluids. She would be kneeling on all fours rocking in pain. Yet when the doctor came she would say she was comfortable.

Mia controlled her medications and opioids and she valued her clarity of mind. When the medications made her drowsy she drank Coke, and although it made her vomit, she seemed to want its stimulation. She requested an intravenous line and fluids. The bag hung on a wooden screen beside her bed. I felt it caused more burden than comfort, for it made the need to walk to the toilet more frequent, as Mia rejected the assistance of a bedpan or catheter. Her moist chest caused painful coughing. Mia was not ready to die just yet. What was keeping her here? Everyone—doctors, nurses, and close friends—were amazed and searched their hearts for any "unfinished business" they could assist Dee with and organize. At this time Mia's brother arrived, and although they had not been close as children, both felt strengthened by their mutual presence. The children's future security was a concern to Mia and she agonized over her will. The final version was prepared and Mia struggled to sit on the side of the bed, and because of increasing blindness, sought assistance with where to sign. This was attended to, yet Mia still struggled for life.

A phone call was received from overseas and that seemed to be the key to releasing the long struggle. Mia relaxed back onto her pillows and died. It was her youngest son's sixth birthday and Mia had made it special for him. As with wanting her children to be free of sexual inhibitions, Mia also wanted her children included in the dying process. When the nurses had dressed her in the special white antique cotton gown she had chosen for this time, the boys put teddy bears on her pillow and lip balm on her lips while remarking, "Mum didn't like to have dry lips." In death Mee still looked stunningly beautiful, and she had squeezed every ounce of life out of her body before discarding it. Rigor mortis set in almost immediately after her breath stopped.

CHAPTER FOUR

Where to Die?

The thought of boys and teddy bears brings me to the story of Gladys. One day I received a phone call from a daughter concerned for her mother, who was a patient in a large teaching hospital. She felt her mother was dying and wanted to take her home. Her father was not keen on the idea and mumbled about the cost. He thought they should leave her in hospital where people knew what to do. I reassured the daughter that the nurses who worked with me were very familiar with the needs of the dying and supported her in honoring the mother/daughter bond. I told the daughter I would be happy to meet with her and her father at the hospital if that would be helpful. It was a long weekend and on Saturday I received a phone call from the daughter. She explained the doctors at the hospital had postponed making any decisions regarding her mother until Tuesday morning. They had, however, removed the intravenous line and ceased medications. The daughter felt Tuesday would be too late to bring her mother home and asked if I could meet them at the hospital that afternoon.

I never find it easy to say "no." Gladys was in a six-bed hospital ward with bed rails in place, and she appeared to be unresponsive during our visit. The nursing staff was welcoming and cooperative as together we considered a possible way forward in honoring the wishes of the daughter and allaying the fears of her father. It was agreed that if an ambulance and a doctor prepared to sign the discharge papers could be found, Gladys could be taken home. This all happened within a short space of time and the daughter's eight-year-old son was permitted to ride in the ambulance with his grandma. It was decided to put Gladys in the front bedroom with matching bedspreads and curtains that were examples of the sewing she used to do. No sooner had Gladys been positioned in her bed, than she requested a cup of tea. This amazed us all, for we thought she was unconscious. My car was the home of emergency supplies, but unfortunately I did not have a bedpan among the many other nursing items. I did have equipment for a catheter and suggested to the daughter that this might be a practical way of avoiding a wet bed and reducing the need to disturb her mother. The young son was an only child and was used to having his questioning mind satisfied with answers. I explained that the leg bag with its non-return valve would be like having a bladder outside the body.

The bedroom became a peaceful scene, as having Mum in her rightful place created a sense of the normal. I noticed that Gladys' husband had swollen feet and ankles and offered to massage them. Questions concerning this swelling were answered and although he grumbled and was cynical, he was reassured. The power of touch conveyed concern for him and also helped to reassure him that Gladys was in good hands. A doctor from the family practice attended and ordered an anxiolytic medication in addition to the pain relieving medication that came from the hospital. Sunday was a relatively peaceful day and spent with photograph albums dotted on the spare bed in the front room. Gladys' son arrived by plane and the family unit was complete. On that Monday afternoon, I received a call asking that I come. Gladys was quietly slipping away, secure in her own homely atmosphere. Her husband, no longer brusque or removed, was holding one hand and her daughter and grandson held another when her breath gently and finally stopped.

After the doctor had been in to confirm death, I explained to the family that I would like to wash Gladys and dress her in a fresh nightdress before calling the funeral people. The grandson asked if he could help. Why not? He chose the nightdress and helped with the basin of water and towels. "Why are you washing her?" he asked. I thought for a moment and replied, "Out of respect for the house she lived in while she was here." We completed our task with respect and privacy and I sent him into the garden to pick some flowers to place in his grandmother's hand, which rested on the homemade bedspread. As it was early in the evening, I asked the daughter and her father if they wanted the funeral people to remove Gladys as soon as possible or if they would like to wait until morning. It was Gladys' husband who made the decision to postpone the event until morning.

Gladys' eight-year-old grandson placed his teddy bear on the chair beside her so she wouldn't be lonely. The atmosphere was one of peace and as I drove home, I thought what a great story the little boy would have to tell at school. At the funeral he was there in his bow tie recording the names of the small gathering, and I knew that his first close experience with death would give him confidence and "know-how" to face future deaths. I reflected on the fact that Tuesday morning in the hospital would have been too late and if the daughter had not been so persistent in her efforts to follow her intuition, circumstances would have been a lot different. I thought of all the times that I had put off making a decision, somehow unconsciously hoping it would not be necessary if I could just wait long enough. I thought of the times when I had made a decision but had not followed my voice of intuition. I remember once putting off a hospital visit that had been on my mind for several days only to find that when I did go, the patient had died several hours earlier. I felt guilty. Since that time I have found my car heading in directions not consciously intended but which turn out to have a purpose.

CHAPTER FIVE

Visitors

Vera was a small, elderly lady suffering from scleroderma. She and her husband came to Australia from their Southern European home as young people. Life in those early days of adjustment to a new culture and language was tough. As Vera was dying, her husband recalled with me how Vera had been a successful milliner and shopkeeper and an active member of community organizations. Together they had raised a large family, and it was this family who taught me about visitors.

The day before Vera died, she had sixty or so visitors. Children, grandchildren, and great grandchildren came to say their good-byes and acknowledge this brave lady in whatever way was dear to their hearts. Propped up on her pillows, Vera had little strength to respond, but she gave each visitor a blink of her eyes in recognition. It was not tiring for her, as is the frequent complaint about visitors. How proud and successful she must have felt as this homage took place.

Just before Vera died, the small room contained her husband, a son from the country town where she had worked so hard, and myself. We were seated around the bed and I was an eager listener to her life as told by these two men. The son recalled how his mother used to feed the members of his football team and put up with attempts at handball with rolled up socks in the corridor of their home. The doctor was called when her temperature began to rise and her breathing became noisy. He seemed not to know how to react to the peaceful scene and, appearing thankful for his stethoscope, proceeded to examine her chest. The almost lifeless body was sat forward and the nightdress was raised. "Lungs filling up with fluid. Probably heart failure. Won't be long," were his mutterings as he left the room to talk outside the door to a family member.

I have always felt uncomfortable with the practice of talking about patients outside the room. It is their life, their body, and their future that are being discussed and, unless the patient has indicated or the death is occurring in a culture where relatives are expected to take over these concerns, I believe that sort of talk must include the patient. It is often said by hospice workers that hearing is the last sense to go. I would like to think that Vera could "hear" the complimentary things said about her, especially during her last days.

When Vera died, the family and friends from their church took over the arrangements and I left, having washed and dressed her. Next day I bumped into her son in the street. I asked him how he felt and he said, "Wonderful. After the funeral people took Mum away, I turned the mattress over and slept in her bed, which was beside Dad's, so that we could be company for each other."

There is, however, a need for the primary caregiver to educate well-meaning visitors so their visits can be helpful for the dying person. The important thing to highlight is that the visitor is the giver of energy and must not sap the diminishing energy of the person who is dying. For example, a visitor may say, "Don't talk, I just want to sit here and reminisce about our school days," or, "I've brought you the first ripe tomato from my garden to smell," or, "I'm just going to sit here and quietly work." Unfortunately, family or caregivers often feel it is easier to keep visitors away than to give the shepherding that they require to fulfill a positive role in the dying process.

CHAPTER SIX

The Anniversary

The very first person to be referred to me when I began to practice as a private palliative care nurse in 1987 was a young mother of two small children. I will call her Margaret. Margaret was a professional woman and had breast cancer. She had chosen to rely on natural therapies until a short time before her death when she was hospitalized and given chemotherapy. I didn't ever meet Margaret personally but was asked to see her brother, sister, and mother. We talked about the need for honest communication and saying good-bye and involving the children.

I remember making the mistake of saying to Margaret's mother, as we talked in the garden of the hospital, that Margaret had packed many activities into her life by experiencing a happy marriage, a successful career, travel, and children. My remarks didn't help the mother, who was grieving for her daughter and was feeling very angry. I must have sounded so trite with this "Pollyanna" approach. Margaret's brother and sister came to visit me in my office and I don't remember what I said to them, but whatever it was came from my heart. After Margaret died, I saw Margaret's mother several times and remember calling with a book for her, hoping that its contents would be more effective than my words. There was so much hurt in the family unit.

A year after Margaret died, I received a phone call from another state and a man's voice said, "I'm Margaret's brother. Do you remember me?" My mind did a rapid rewind to visualize this young, sensitive man who was struggling to find his niche in a world far removed from his parents' expectations and who had sought to find meaning in his sister's death. The voice on the phone continued, "It is the anniversary of Margaret's death and I just want to tell you what has happened to me since then. You told me at the time that I could make Margaret's death the best or worst thing that has happened to me, and I just want to tell you that it is the best thing that has happened to me. My career as a commercial artist is just taking off, I'm married, and the birth of our first child is imminent. Most importantly, I feel Margaret's presence and guidance constantly with me."

I was taken aback to think that I said such words, and I don't think that I could consciously say today that a death could be the best or worst thing in a person's life. I certainly acknowledge the power of positive thinking and that a person has a choice as to how they choose to react to life events. We don't choose the events that life presents us with, but we can choose how we respond to them. Many years later at an anniversary time, I heard from Margaret's brother again. This time was to tell me of his continued success in the commercial world and that as a family they had been to the cemetery to visit Margaret's memorial.

Anniversaries are important times for sifting through the maze of emotions which surface. Grief and bereavement programs pay special attention to anniversaries, and computers are making the thoughtful act of a contact at this time easier to facilitate. Now I listen to stories of funeral homes having memorial services and giving people who attend a potted plant of rosemary as a symbol to be personally interpreted. Most hospice programs facilitate bereavement programs and invite the families and friends of their patients to a memorial service. Today I also see many nursing homes conducting memorial services for families or a special afternoon tea for staff that were involved in a caring role.

Successful grieving is hard work for the individual, and the process can be facilitated by a professional primary caregiver as part of the separation process. I have found that a special bonding takes place between the people who share the experience of a person's death and that the professional primary caregiver involved at the time is a valuable asset in supporting those who have been involved. Grieving begins before death and continues after death. It is an important process for realizing the significance of the relationship that has been lost and how it has shaped our spiritual nature.

CHAPTER SEVEN

Music and Photographs

I first met Marion in a small private hospital where she was biding her time. Her doctor and some members of her family wanted her transferred to a hospice, but one of her sons who lived in the country felt his mother would be more at peace at home. Marion had secondaries in her lungs from cancer and, apart from being breathless, she was not in physical pain. The pain she felt was in her psyche, and once her hospital bed was made for the day her main activity was choosing her daily diet from a hospital menu and looking at the tiny screen of a television suspended above her bed. Nurses buzzed in and out of the room with their various tasks but the important issues in Marion's life were unaddressed until the doctor went on holidays and the son was able to persuade his replacement that his mother would be better off at home. People who purported to know best thought this was an impossible idea as Marion lived alone. However, where there is a will there is a way, and Marion herself was keen to be able to say good-bye to her home and all her treasures.

The discharge took place and the first morning I saw Marion at home, I found her sitting in the garden fondly looking at the hanging baskets and garden beds. She was dressed and wore bright red stockings. I can still see them in my mind and recall being amazed at the different person she was. Home turf can do wonders in giving a person a sense of being in control. A light was set next to the bed and a neighbor was alerted to heed its signal. The son came on the weekends from the country, sometimes accompanied by his wife and children and sometimes alone. A nurse visited daily to help with her shower and bed making and to provide a listening ear.

It was Marion's wish to visit her daughter who lived in another state, and her son set aside time to go with her. Before leaving, Marion organized her funeral. Her son took a bottle of opiate mixture in case of discomfort and bravely accompanied his mother in the airplane. On Marion's return to Adelaide, it was evident that her life was limited. In spite of the frequent massaging with aromatherapy oils, it was more and more difficult for Marion to get her legs to work. Her spirit was indeed willing but, like Mia, her body was failing. During the last week of her life some very precious events took place. The nurse was shown the bedside drawer, which contained little parcels, each bearing the name of a grandchild. As toileting was difficult and distressing, a urinary drainage catheter provided relief from the effort. I remember making a joke about the drainage bag as I tucked it into a knitting bag for privacy as we prepared for a last play of her favorite card game with her regular group of friends. It was a mighty effort and the laughter around the table did little to prepare those friends for Marion's death just days later.

The night before she died, Marion sat up in bed and sipped champagne through a straw. Her son had brought the glass to the bedside on a wooden tray he had made at school. How can a hospital or hospice compete with that atmosphere? As Marion lay dying, her old gramophone dance tunes were played continuously and seemed to bring her a contented smile. There was a lot of massage of the areas on the soles of Marion's feet that represent the lungs and very little medication was needed. For the last twelve hours or so, injections of opioid were given—three to four hourly—but I feel the most important contributing factor to Marion's comfort was the state of her mind. When her breath stopped, her son was by the bedside and observed a tear escaping from his mother's eye. This was a symbol to be personally interpreted.

When I had washed and dressed Marion, her son indicated that he wished he could photograph her, and I remember taking a battery out of my pager so that this could happen. It all seemed so natural at the time and while a flower on her pillow signified her love of the garden, an even more significant thought was to enter the mind of her son. When the funeral people came, the son accompanied his mother's coffin down the driveway of the house and remarked on the sunset, "Mum was from the country and leaving us at sunset seems most appropriate." The rest of the family gathered for the funeral and, after the service, returned to the house, where the dining room table was covered with photographs that honored Marion's life, the establishment of her city garden, and the photograph taken after her death. Some people thought this photo was in poor taste but the son, who knew his mother so well, felt it was part of the whole. That was in 1988 and now it is common to photograph people in their coffins or before the funeral people take them away.

CHAPTER EIGHT

Death as a Long Journey

Photographing the coffin reminds me of Bill, who died in 1995. His dying was a marathon. He had cancer of his throat and required a tracheotomy to breathe. Bill lived alone and for years had fought cancer by way of much surgery. When I met him, he was surrounded by his three sons and their wives. He was proudly sitting in a recliner chair that his children had bought and a very voluptuous nude dominated the wall of the small room. Speech was difficult for Bill and it required a trained ear to understand what he was trying to say.

I had been asked to come because the family didn't know how to best help Bill. Everyone wanted to be supportive but they needed a trained person as their guide. I often think about life as a journey and, like all journeys, when the way is unfamiliar it is reassuring to have a knowing guide alongside. With a guide, the countryside—of nature or emotions—can be examined and appreciated, secure in the knowledge that practical issues are being taken care of en route. I would pose a question and Bill would respond with some indication of his wishes. He indicated that he didn't believe in a life after death and that he wanted to stay at home to die. Fortunately some private health insurance was available to assist with nurse visits and the sons took turns sleeping in the house at night. Bill cleaned his own tracheotomy tube and used a blender to prepare his food. A large block of chocolate with its blue wrapper was always on the table. Bill's pride and joy was his waterbed, which did not make for easy nursing. The only way to do the necessary nursing tasks was for me to climb onto the bed and ride the swell as best I could.

One evening the boys were gathered and I needed to attend to an injection line that was giving Bill a mixture of medication in the struggle to keep him comfortable. Every time we touched the weeping wound dressings around his neck or tried to clean around the tracheotomy tube from which foul smelling discharge spewed with every breath, Bill's face became distorted with pain. This particular evening, after changing the site of the needle, I lay back on the bed beside him after the struggle to keep steady, and continued to listen to the stories about the photographs, which were kept in a wooden box on top of the wardrobe. Suddenly one of the boys started to laugh and said, "If Dad looks down and sees Joy beside him on the bed, he is never going to want to leave." The atmosphere around the bed was good as we looked at the very old photographs of the many cars that had been Bill's absorbing interest. He had worked for a car manufacturer and was proud of his gold watch, which represented many years of faithful service.

Since the breakup of his marriage, Bill had taken an interest in various women, including the local barmaid. He had apparently demonstrated to his sister that he had a "curl-the-mo" nurse. "Curl-the-mo" or not, I was to learn a great deal from Bill. Our mutual acceptance of each other grew as I collected Bill in my car and took him for radiotherapy and doctors' visits. There were lots of moments of merriment in our interactions. One day as I was driving Bill home, I overshot his street and when Bill tapped me on the arm to communicate, I realized what I had done and asked, "Why didn't you shout at me?" He grinned as he pointed to his tracheotomy. Other times I would say, "There is no point in us trying to talk to each other in this traffic so I will just play a cassette tape, okay?" Humor is a very useful tool for conveying emotional messages that are difficult to express and Bill loved a ribbing.

The first evening I met Bill and his family, it was discovered that constipation was a problem that needed to be addressed. Allan was the son who was to play a major role in the nursing of his father and we agreed to meet with the new local doctor the next evening. As the doctor was delayed and I had another appointment, I explained to Allan how to insert the suppository, which hopefully would stimulate some action in the bowel department. Allan listened for a while and then said with a grin, "It is all right, Joy. I will just say: Dad, trust me!" To Bill, Allan said something such as, "You are not going to like this. I am not going to like it either, so let's just get on with it!" Bill was a down-to-earth working bloke and appreciated a pragmatic approach.

The time from when Bill became unconscious and stopped taking food to the day he died was three weeks. Since Bill's face was full of frowns when we tried to clean his tracheotomy or attend to the care of his hygiene and skin, his medications included a sedative as well as pain relief. This state of sleep and relaxation was disturbed several times during the three-week period when Bill suddenly woke up, sat up, and wanted to give his family hugs. Everyone was keen for the suffering to end and as a divided family that gradually came together, we all wondered what was going on at a deeper level for this dying man. One day I phoned to hear Allan say with great pleasure that Mum was back in the kitchen and was cooking and cleaning the house she had left some ten years before. Bill even puckered up his lips for a kiss for this hard-working woman who had been a part of his life for so many years.

Bill's body began to feed on itself and we were constantly amazed at the amount of urine that was collected via uridome drainage. (We had only to experience one wet waterbed to realize that an uridome and leg bag was the way to go.) Bill's own mother came back into the picture, as did his brothers and sisters. The lady across the road who had been a good friend supplied linen and another listening ear. So much healing of hurt feelings was taking place around the man who was lying on his waterbed spewing foul discharge from a hole in his neck. We wondered what else was going on and Allan suggested that in spite of Bill's protests that when you are dead you are dead; maybe some prayers from a minister would help. That is how the hospice chaplain was invited to visit. This was felt to be successful but still Bill's psyche seemed to need time to heal. I believe that just as the physical body has the resources to heal itself, so does the psyche, and just as doctors, nurses, and caregivers can assist the physical body, so too can those who understand a transpersonal influence be helpful to the psyche. A lot of "spooky" things happen at the time of death and, in Bill's case, the events that unfolded were phenomenal.

On considering the amount of medication Bill was having, the lack of food and fluids, and the general state of his body and the organs that were gradually shutting down, we came to the conclusion that he would die when he was ready and that was that. However, we were all getting very tired and the boys' home life and the time spent with their own children were suffering. Some evenings all would gather for a meal in the tiny house and on several occasions I felt privileged to be included. Beer was Bill's drink and one night the boys and Bill's brother went to the local pub and positioned themselves, as Bill would have, at the counter. In honor of his memory they bought a bingo ticket. It won them a few dollars and was placed in Bill's hand when he was in his coffin—along with the nude painting and a toy pink elephant.

One evening, the two youngest boys, on impulse, poured gasoline on the back lawn to form a cross and the words "home," "Bill," and the names of the family members. The letters and symbol were set alight and when "V" was the last to go out, the boys contemplated its meaning and said, "Victory!" Reactions are personal, and this play may have seemed irresponsible to some but it helped to ease the mounting tension, as did their actions one night when they were telling me about their dad's love of cars with V8 motors. It was decided to juggle a few of the cars in the driveway and park Allan's V8 motor under the window of Bill's bedroom and rev it up. They thought Dad would love it and were sure that he heard the familiar sounds. "He could tell a V8 anywhere," they assured me. Allan would speak to his dad encouragingly, "You are on the highway now, Dad. Open it up and let it go."

Still Bill did not die. The medications were increased, as there was no way of knowing how efficiently his body was able to metabolize them. The prime intention was to prevent suffering if at all possible. Allan, who at that time had a lawn mowing business, became an expert at giving injections as well as an expert at cleaning the tracheotomy stoma, which was becoming distorted by the tumor. He told me several months after his father died that the night of the setting the lawn alight, he had received a clear message that he was to train as a nurse and "help Joy in her work."

On the morning of Bill's death, I had changed the smelly dressings and tried to shave Bill to make him as dignified as possible. He was being nursed on a medical woolen overlay to prevent pressure sores, and everyone who went to the bedside was encouraged to move the waterbed because, unless the pressure was changing, the water surface would be "hard" and damage to the skin could occur rapidly. While I hated to disturb Bill for nursing procedures, as they raised his level of consciousness and produced agitation, these procedures were necessary and done as quickly as possible. This particular morning my nursing attention provided a level of consciousness for a valuable exchange between Allan and his father. Allan asked Bill, as he had many times before, if he was ready to die. There was a very definite nod of the head and those around the bed wondered what more we could do to help this long, protracted dying process. The family suggested the hospice doctor be asked to visit.

How often calls to the doctor are made when people feel helpless and powerless. As we didn't know what time the doctor would arrive, Allan went about his lawn mowing business but stopped when a tightening of his throat reminded him to phone Bill's home. He found a public phone and received the news that the doctor was on his way. I arrived after the doctor's visit to find Bill much more comfortable, as medications for pain relief and sedation had been increased, and all the boys were present. It had been a struggle to walk that particular journey and try to juggle all the emotions that had surfaced. Watching the body become a skeleton with a rib cage falling sharply to an abdomen that looked like it had been sucked in by a vacuum pump was not easy.

Yet if death had occurred sooner, there would not have been the opportunity for many relationships to heal. What I'm trying to say is that there seemed to be some meaning in Bill's suffering. It seemed that he was being given a choice and a chance to change things. One night Allan's car was stolen and found at the bottom of a cliff. I imagined that this somehow was a warning: "Don't take over and crash my vehicle (Bill's body) like yours was taken over and crashed." Bill's workmates "whipped around the hat" for a donation in Bill's memory and many attended the funeral service, which was led by the priest who had come to the home to say prayers for those ready to receive them.

It is difficult to find words to "soften" death. "Transition" is a word coined by Dr. Elisabeth Kubler-Ross, the Swiss psychiatrist who taught us so much about new attitudes toward death and dying. Another expression, which I learned from a Roman Catholic nun, is, "Death is just a terminus for the soul to change vehicles." At the Elisabeth Kubler-Ross "Life, Death, and Transition" workshop I attended in 1988, she told us that she believed that with "transition" there is "all knowledge" of how our thoughts, words, and deeds have affected our own life and the lives of those we came in contact with while we lived. This recalling of a life reminds me of Eastern religions such as Buddhism, which suggest an individual path to enlightenment whereby all actions have a reaction or "as you sow, so shall you reap" from the Christian tradition.

CHAPTER NINE

The Voice Beyond

In order to maintain confidentiality, our nurses often give their patients special names. Mrs. Bunny was ninety-eight years old when we were invited to assist in her care. She was a woman of high birth and was privately educated by tutors. Her mind was as sharp as a tack but her heart was failing and her spine had taken the shape of her pillows. She liked to sit bolt upright in bed, and for many years her bed had become her special domain. From the bed she rang the bell to summon her faithful housekeeper, who was well trained in Mrs. Bunny's ways of doing things. Her efforts to keep up her standards of living were great and I remember that her tray had to be set "just so."

I loved taking a turn in caring for Mrs. Bunny. The bed bath was only performed three times a week, for the procedure was exhausting. The towels and fresh nightdress were warmed, the room was warmed, and her toilet things were set out on a trolley. These items included salt water for the douche of a specific temperature, the cream for her face (soap and water were never allowed near her face!), face washes, body washing cloths, protective hydrocolloid gel dressing to protect the ear from the pressure of her glasses, talcum powder and a puff for its application, cotton buds for cleaning the ears and umbilicus, and alcohol swabs for drying between the toes— just as the basics. From time to time, padding was added to protect the spine, which was becoming red and broken from pressure on the pillows, as well as the necessary equipment for an enema or suppository and the hydrocolloid dressings, just coming into use, to protect the sacral area. There was a routine for changing the bed linen and very specific placement of the pillows was needed to prevent the little bell from ringing. Frequent struggling on and off her slipper bedpan to prevent "an accident" was exhausting for Mrs. Bunny and difficult for one person to achieve with her. Watching the pennies was important for Mrs. Bunny; hence household help and nursing care were kept to a minimum. (I have found that so many people wish they were able to budget for their death at a known date.)

One night Mrs. Bunny called the NurseLink Helpline twenty-four hour number in the early hours of the morning and told me she had spilt a glass of water in her bed and asked if I would come and help her. I had been summoned and went with good grace but charged for an after-hours call-out visit. Money matters and being paid for work performed rather than working for a salary and set hours is something new to the majority of nurses. Rising costs, industrial regulations, "servants" wanting a life to call their own, and reduced exposure to the outside world were all factors which now affected the care Mrs. Bunny felt she needed to stay in her own home. "Don't put me in hospital," were words often expressed as she battled with her failing heart, a urinary infection from the indwelling catheter, which she appreciated, and pneumonia. The doctor came regularly and he had promised his patient that when she died he would make sure that she was indeed dead before letting her be taken away. This was one of her fears, along with fears of not being able to control her own life and losing her mind. Mrs. Bunny had no children of her own so the family who came to support her included mostly nieces and nephews. Visitors were often sent away if it did not suit Mrs. Bunny to receive them. In fact, we were all a bit scared of her.

Even in death she terrified me, although I felt it a great privilege to be with her the night that she died.

One day as I was dressing Mrs. Bunny's back and her face was turned away from me, I dared to ask a personal question. Before starting the dressing she had asked me why I was looking so tired. I told her that I had been up all night with a forty-year-old man who was dying of a brain tumor. "I don't want to hear about it," was Mrs. Bunny's reaction. But I suspected that she did want to talk about dying and had questions concerning her own death, yet this was a topic, like so many others, that was forbidden in "nice" circles. I told her this young man had wanted to take his tablets all at once so that he wasn't a burden on his family. I asked, "When you are tired of living, do you think that you would like to control the timing of your death?" There was silence and I thought that I would not be forgiven for the risk I was taking in trying to bring up an unmentionable subject. As I gently righted this small, frail lady, she fixed me with her eye and said, "I thought about what you said and I want to live because I want to live and I'll just wait for the chopper."

Several months before Mrs. Bunny's one hundredth birthday, I asked her if she was going to make "one hundred" and her reply was, "It all depends on how hot the summer is, Joy." After her birthday a decision had to be made about the special draw sheets, which absorb moisture that we needed to put on her bed. She asked me if I thought it wise to buy them or to rent them. I replied that if she was going to die in a few weeks' time I would rent them, but if she was going to live for another fourteen years I would advise her to buy them. She looked at me with a twinkle in her eye and said, "I'll buy!" We had a special relationship that had grown over the years but I felt that I was still on trial.

For some time Mrs. Bunny had been commenting on how heavy her feet were becoming and one evening as her nurse was settling her for the night, Mrs. Bunny asked to be carried upstairs. She may have been remembering her childhood, when as a little girl she was carried upstairs to her bedroom. I like to think she was preparing to be carried up to another "bedroom."

On the morning of her death, Mrs. Bunny was very breathless and becoming distressed. The doctor asked what I thought we needed to do. I said that I thought an opioid injection would make her more comfortable. "Interesting" was the doctor's reply. He added, "I don't know that she has ever had any, so perhaps we should give her something to prevent nausea before the injection." These medications were given and a peaceful, restful day ensued with a few favorite visitors. (There needs to be a good rapport between nurse and doctor, and as a nurse I appreciate the responsibilities that doctors face. If the nurse can be supportive as well as being a patient advocate, a valuable trusting relationship can develop, and the nurse and doctor roles can be complementary.)

Later in the day I was having a meal on a tray beautifully prepared by the housekeeper when there was a change in Mrs. Bunny's breathing. I felt for her pulse, knowing that she had died. The doctor came and thoroughly listened for a heartbeat and held a mirror under her nose to detect the faintest sign of a breath. I think he felt, like I did, that she was up in the ceiling making sure he carried out her wishes.

Several months before Mrs. Bunny died, she did have her hundredth birthday and was the charming hostess to a large party. She was so proud of her telegrams from the Queen and Australian Prime Minister. Her nightdress and bed jacket had been chosen with care for the birthday event, and it was with these clothes that I was to dress her after death. It was such a good feeling to be able to move her body without causing pain and I set about removing her clothes and washing her. I had a face washer in my hand, wet with soap and water, and was about to wash her face when I became aware of what I was doing, thinking, "Don't!" Oh, my god! I had almost put the soap and water on her face that she had avoided all her adult life and forgot her preferred cream. I felt her presence strongly as I made her look stately on her pillows. I wondered how the funeral people would cope with the shape of her body in a coffin. The relatives agreed that a nurse should stay in the house with her for the night. It would not have seemed proper in any way to hurry her away.

CHAPTER TEN

In the Hospital Setting

I had been asked by a medical oncologist to visit Rene in her private hospital room to talk about going home for terminal care. While we talked, I had a sense of the great wall this small lady was building around herself. She seemed starved for tenderness and touch and didn't want to go home, for it was evident that there were painful memories of home. At the same time she didn't want to sound as though she wasn't keen to go home, for that would have been the expected reaction and Rene was well versed in the "right" way to behave. Because Rene had difficulty in breathing and relied on oxygen, her back and bottom were becoming numb from sitting upright. I thought a back rub might afford an opportunity for some nonverbal communication between us. The massage was extended to her feet, and I spoke about reflexology and the different areas of the foot that may assist her breathing. I told her I would visit again if she wanted me to and was reassured by the oncologist that my visit would be welcome because Rene liked "that Chinese stuff."

As I massaged Rene's feet, we talked about our children and the coincidence of their going to the same swimming club. When I tried to talk about possible discharge arrangements or palliative care topics the wall went up, so I stopped and concentrated on grandchildren and family topics. I met her children and they were keen to be supportive in whatever way possible. It was some time before I met Rene's husband, who was quite a hero in his own way, as he had rehabilitated himself following an accident from a wheelchair existence to walking. As we all continued to get to know each other, it was evident that Rene's husband had been the dominating force at home. Maybe that was why she needed her own space in hospital. For whatever reason, Rene didn't go home and spent her days in the hospital, and during the last few weeks I would visit most days and massage her feet. That was mostly all I did. I tried to talk about her spiritual needs and she said she used to enjoy going to church but it wasn't her husband's cup of tea so church had not been a recent part of her life—and no, she didn't want a minister to visit. I knew Rene had attended meditation classes and I tried to talk about that but again I heard, "I don't want to talk about it."

Sometimes Rene would sit for an hour in a chair in her hospital room adjoining a garden and I would pull up a stool and put a towel on my lap and proceed to massage her feet. One day she said, "I'm not much company for you. I just go to sleep on you." I replied, "Actually it is quite an honor that you feel so comfortable in my presence that you can go to sleep." One day a doctor friend came to visit. Rene had been his receptionist for many years and this visit was very much appreciated. Her years of being his receptionist provided another topic for us to talk about.

One day I was allowed to give Rene an enema. With the lack of exercise—just getting in and out of bed was a huge effort and took all her energy—and the introduction of oral pain-relieving medication, Rene's constipation was making her uncomfortable. Because the upright position was her favorite, an extra layer of foam and alternating pressure mattress were added to the bed. Pressure points were becoming a problem. After her bowels were cleared, Rene agreed to a catheter so that the energy required to get onto the commode chair could instead be spent with visitors and admiring the room full of flowers and the sunlit garden outside. I sensed it was time for Rene to stay in bed and was surprised when I returned after a weekend break to find her sitting out of bed again. It was as though we had had a little rehearsal but she wasn't ready to "let go" just yet.

When Rene did become too weak to leave her bed, she allowed me to feed her and I knew this was indeed a privilege. I even got to clean her teeth one day as this independent person and I continued on a path of mostly nonverbal close communication. One day I told her that I had to go to another state for a visit and wouldn't be able to see her for several weeks. She said, "Only three more days." We both knew she was dying and since I couldn't bring myself to say good-bye to her the day before I left, I visited her again on the way to the airport. This time she was scarcely conscious and I told her who I was, gave her a kiss on the forehead, and said, "Bloody hell, you have to be dying before you allow anyone to show you affection. Be that ship on the horizon that goes out of sight but doesn't vanish." A smile crossed her face and there was a look of utmost peace as she said, "Joy, it is all a myth." I was held spellbound in the moment and ever since I have realized my missed opportunity. What is a myth? This life, life after death, or whatever? Rene was in a peaceful place where the questions she wouldn't reveal to me or to her psychologist, who also visited, were being answered. I flew to my destination and that night in the early hours of the morning was awake and thinking of Rene. I remember getting up and noting the time. When I arrived at the office later in the morning I was told that Rene had died in the night—at the time I was disturbed. I like to think she figuratively touched me on the shoulder as she passed by on the horizon crossing.

CHAPTER ELEVEN

What to Wear?

Molly, like Rene, died in a room of a private hospital. When I met her she was sitting up in bed scratching her hairless head. One of the nurses introduced us and left us to talk. Talk we did, for unlike Rene, Molly was like a tight spring that had just been released. In the first few minutes, I was told of an event that had obviously weighed heavily on Molly's mind and probably contributed to her illness. My brief this time was to prepare Molly for a meditation retreat center where cancer sufferers are helped with healthy ways of eating and using their minds, with a focus on turning the illness around. Sometimes, as I massaged her body parts that were not covered with dressings or tight clothing, I played relaxation music and talked. Sometimes we both listened to a guided imagery cassette tape and let the tape dictate the timing of the massage strokes.

These visits and chats went on over a period of some months, with Molly getting to the retreat center and spending time in her country home. She made arrangements and tried to finish her work with stained glass windows. Molly and I would talk about golf, which had given enjoyment to both of us, her woodwork, her family—two sons, one doctor daughter, many grandchildren, and a close sister—and her life as a country child who was sent to board with a number of families while she attended school. The stories of childhood, which surface at times of life review, are numerous, and it is no wonder that there are "heal the hurt child" schools of thought as people seek self-knowledge. Gandhi has been reported to have written on a paper bag, "My message is my life," for a man who was running beside his train as it pulled out of an African station and who asked for a message to take home to his village.

When Molly died she was in the private room in the private hospital where she had spent months in the past year. One day I received a phone call from Molly's daughter, who said that her brother was due to arrive and she was concerned that her mother would be upset, as contact between them had been minimal since a misunderstanding concerning a loan of money. I am reminded of Shakespeare's wise words spoken in *Hamlet* by Polonius: "Neither a borrower nor a lender be, for loan oft loses both itself and friend, and borrowing dulls the edge of husbandry."

Money is an issue for division in so many family relationships. I would often say that there is no pocket in a shroud. A Catholic priest who had spent time with Mother Teresa of Calcutta told me of this saying of hers; "The poor are rich in spirit but the rich are often poor in spirit." As it is the soul carried on energy that leaves the body, the quest for money alone seems to me to be an unworthy goal. Molly's daughter asked me if I could be present when her brother arrived. Mother and son greeted each other warmly and it was a meeting that needed to happen. Photographs and a letter from the son's children were placed alongside the others in the room. Another son arrived and that evening I was invited into the hospital room for a champagne supper. There are more ways than one to share "communion," which is pivotal to organized Christian religion. I felt that the atmosphere in that room at that mealtime was one of healing, forgiveness, and togetherness. I feel that it is a part of good palliative care to celebrate life and encourage an atmosphere of love and even laughter.

As Molly lay dying, her sister also arrived and hoped that she would be able to stay for the funeral. This reminds us that the time of death becomes an issue when we look at the greater good of having the needs of those left behind taken into consideration. The funeral is a formal way of saying good-bye and makes the separation an experienced reality. Many times relatives from other parts of the country or world are denied this, and often this is because of medical interventions such as continuing with oxygen or giving intravenous nutrition, which may prolong the dying process. There is a need for much understanding and feeling comfortable with the dying process on the part of all health professionals. The question often raised is, "If as a society we can use technology to prolong life, can it also be a tool for shortening what has been prolonged?" Where is God and fate in all this? Is it God's will that the particular caregivers, who are bent on preserving life at all costs, should continue to care for a particular person and prolong life while what the psyche needed to achieve has been achieved? Or is it God's will that the caregivers in a particular life are sent because they are comfortable with the transition about to take place and won't panic and seek to set in place technologies which would interfere with the natural dying process?

Many family and friends who seek to walk the journey with a dying person lose confidence at a crucial moment and call an ambulance. The result is often that the person dies in the ambulance. Molly didn't die in an ambulance but rather was surrounded by her family, having had a blessing from a favorite minister who, at the funeral, knowingly described Molly as a friend who was like a woolen vest—she was warm but prickly at times. Death occurred at 11:00 PM, and the daughter and I took our time to shampoo and blow dry Molly's new growth of hair after chemotherapy, wash her, and dress her. Her clothes were chosen by her daughter and had been brought down from Molly's country home in readiness. They were glamorous from the underwear to the top and skirt. During the three-hour process there were many tears and many spoken good-byes and questions, and the hospital staff were pleased that I was there, as their time allocation for individual patients was limited.

Working together is what works best. I have known situations where the hospital staff resent the fact that an outsider can have the time and closeness with their patients when they can't. Organizations and individuals are often inward looking and there can be an attitude of wanting to build up a good reputation for their own team and their own way of doing things. This type of care is organization-centered rather than patient-centered, where the individual is all-important.

In the early hours of the morning, Molly's daughter and I went home for a rest, only to return with her sons at 8:00 AM. They were both smiling with a private joke at the expense of the domestic staff, who had asked if their mother, whom we had left ready for the funeral people to collect, wanted breakfast! It was time to clear the room, pack up Molly's personal belongings, and say good-bye to the hospital staff, who had all been touched by this death in their ward.

CHAPTER TWELVE

Who Inherits?

It was a second marriage for Fred, and he was just beginning to enjoy life after his first wife's death when he was diagnosed with cancer and secondaries in his bones. Fred liked to organize and control. He was a valuable member of his bowls club and he kept their books for them. When I met him he was organizing the repair and painting of his house and his wife was keen for him to sort out his will and make peace with his children. His spirit was willing but his level of physical pain prevented him from doing the tasks at hand. He was reluctant to hire others to do jobs that he could do so well himself. When his pain became controlled, he falsely believed that the problem no longer existed and that he could now climb ladders and paint the house. This is an example of how pain is often useful for personal safety. The pain had prevented him climbing a ladder and twisting and reaching. Without the pain, such actions could result in fractures of the bone already weakened with cancer. Fred accepted this warning and turned to more realistic tasks, such as finding the address of his son who was living overseas. A simple restructure of the living room and a telephone extension cord enabled Fred to be in touch with tradesmen and members of his bowls club.

With the introduction of pain relieving medication, bowel problems presented themselves. This bothered Fred considerably, and diet and oral laxatives did not work for him. He was extremely pleased with the instant results obtained from an oil and water enema and for the introduction of a regime of laxatives and diet, which considered nausea and pain relief. The desire to regain his strength was ever present and a plastic cushion that enabled his feet to transfer air from one side to another gave him the satisfaction of working his muscles. He tried relaxation tapes but they weren't for him. He did, however, do a lot of talking about the past and his life.

The highlight of Fred's life was his time in the Air Force; he loved the uniform, his mates, and the structure. He admitted that he felt cheated when the war ended and he had to return to his wife and two children and face the responsibilities of being the breadwinner and a family member. He expected his son to perform and accept his orders as those under him had done in the Air Force. Naturally it didn't work and alienation had occurred. His daughter was more forgiving. Fred's first wife died from cancer. Now he was evaluating his own life and he wanted to make contact with his son. This we did achieve via an international phone call. His present wife knew how important the Air Force had been to Fred and following his death she placed his Air Force cap on his coffin.

It was important for Fred and his wife to sort out their wills, for there were two families involved and several properties. This was a difficult time, for the making of a will to some is an admission of defeat and a sign that they are preparing to die. It was especially difficult for Fred, as he needed to contact his own son who had been hurt when he hadn't lived up to his father's expectations all those years ago. Who inherits? Is the present wife more entitled than children from a previous marriage? Agreements need to be made ahead of time in an unemotional and rational environment.

CHAPTER THIRTEEN

The Importance of Symbols and Ritual

Meaningful objects placed on the coffin go beyond words. I remember one woman who decorated her husband's coffin with fronds from his tomato bushes, which had been one of his passions. The bushes had produced fruit to be enjoyed as well as providing all the benefits associated with gardening. When my nursing tutor died, her red cape adorned her coffin and signified to those attending the funeral a life of service. The daughter of a woman nearing death occupied much of the vigil time sewing a silver ribbon around the white velvet shroud for her mother. My brother began his working life on a pineapple farm and his coffin was decorated with baby pineapples as well his mother's favorite Geraldton wax flowers. Photographs are a common sight, as well as memorabilia related to sporting interests and religious symbols.

Sometimes family members have formed a guard of honor from the front door to the vehicle waiting to take the person who has died to the funeral home. Some have added flowers as the trolley, carrying a precious load, made its way. One woman put her husband's tweed hat on the stretcher carrying his body to the transfer vehicle. A daughter ran after the vehicle taking her mother's body to the funeral home and returned quite distraught as a long buried feeling of abandonment returned vividly. This was the memory of herself as a three-year-old child being left at a babysitter's house by her mother for the first time. Now her mother was leaving again and the future was uncomfortable.

Rituals have included family members opening a bedroom window to allow the soul to leave. One particularly poignant ritual followed a funeral service in the person's home. As the coffin was being driven away, a homing pigeon was released. It circled the house three times before following the funeral car.

Music is another soul connection to be thoughtfully chosen for a time of transition. Jane was almost sixty when she died of cancer. Her two daughters had been very supportive of cancer treatments of all kinds for their mother. It was not a battle to be won. One of the daughters was in advertising and captured a stirring tune with a "You can do it, Mum" message made especially for her. As their mother was dying, they filled the room with peaceful, relaxing music. A priest had administered "last rites" and was sitting by the bed. I was supporting the pillows in an upright position to make breathing easier. We all felt each gurgled intake of air and wished there would be a final one. The atmosphere in this emotionally charged bedroom changed dramatically when one of the daughters suggested playing the tune that had been made especially for her. When this rousing, encouraging tune was nearing the end of its three minutes, a complete change occurred. It was as though a cork was released from a bottle. Only this time it was a soul released from a body no longer able to support it. The woman's eyes rolled back and she was gone.

Reading a passage from a holy text to the person who had died is a ritual that has comforted many. One woman told me that she slept on her husband's side of bed because that was where she could feel close to him. Another woman told me that she still sets the table for two and at meal times feels a connection with her late husband in the world of thought.

CHAPTER FOURTEEN

A Good Death

Jean was ninety-three when she died. I had cared for her with a team of assistants for ten months. This journey had many ups and downs but in the end Jean died in character. In the beginning it appeared as if Jean had had a stroke and some damage to her brain. She had vision disturbance, and she was forgetful and very frightened. She had trouble processing conversation and requested we all speak slowly. She made it quite clear that she did not want to go to hospital and wanted to end her life in her own home and in control. Her general practitioner wanted to send her to hospital—the easy solution. Her family was supportive of Jean's wishes and we agreed to seek a referral to a palliative care specialist who would visit at home. She had six children and, when they were young, a housekeeper.

The palliative care specialist visited several times, and Jean felt sufficiently supported by her team of palliative care assistants (who attended her twenty-four hours a day) to continue her life and in particular to gain control of her life as much as she could. She refused walking aids and just wanted to rest her hand on the arm of her assistants. She enjoyed ringing her little brass bell to summon her special caregivers. She had always self-medicated, as she was a nurse before marrying her general practitioner husband. She came to rely on her sleeping pills and her anti-anxiety tablets. Her cough mixture contained codeine and this was another prop she used at times. When a new general practitioner, who would do home visits, was found, Jean attended the surgery for minor complaints such as the removal of lesions on her face. Her appearance was very important to her.

One of the discomforts Jean suffered was arthritis in her joints and, in particular, in her left knee. For this an anti-inflammatory was ordered. Another of her concerns was her atrial fibrillation when her pulse would race and the lack of oxygen supply to her brain caused her to be cognitively impaired. It was also felt that some dementia was present, as she was quite forgetful of people and events at times. Apart from being self-determining, she told me of her one time faith in the Catholic Church. There was a time when she felt that she would like to return to this part of her life but had decided that her spiritual guidance came from within. I was studying clinical hypnosis for much of the time I was Jean's nurse and I would invite her to go to her favorite place in nature whenever she felt the need to feel safe and secure.

So it was that Jean's life progressed. She went to the hairdresser for color and curls. She had her nails painted and these appointments determined her week's activities. She enjoyed consulting her diary before agreeing to an activity. A daughter came every Friday for lunch and to do her shopping. Other children popped in to visit. She often rose to the occasion and certainly made their last family Christmas an event to be remembered. She would take an instant dislike to some members of her caring team and request they be replaced. Again this was her right and was respected, although it was difficult to anticipate. In no way did she wish to be treated like a typical nursing home patient and be spoken to like a child who needed to do what she was told. Even as she entered the last phase of her life and the doctor suggested a catheter for bladder control, she said it was uncomfortable and I was ordered to remove it, which I did.

Jean had had many interests in her life, which included golf, tennis, travel, and playing bridge. The latter became a trial, as her partners were aware of her failing mental activity. For several weeks she played a restricted game with one of her assistants. This too was abandoned when it caused more stress than pleasure and only reminded her of her failing health. She ate like a sparrow but wanted to have a say in what she was served, and if it was not to her liking she said so. For example, the soup had too many bits of vegetable, the sandwiches were not right, and the baking too much or too little. Toward the end, one daughter remembered that she liked junket and this was made for her. Food was for nostalgia, not for nutrition. It also enforced a sense of being in charge of her own life.

Jean's clothes were cared for as well as her many pairs of shoes. This may not seem like a nursing duty, but the clothes were wonderful prompts for remembering special events and the feelings associated with those events. The caring team was careful not to ask questions but to instigate activities as though they had been requested. Jean could always say "no" and this was a risk, but it was better than having a situation where her failing brain had difficulty in working out the answer to a question which made her feel foolish, incompetent, and invariably angry. Conversation revolved around her loved ones, the swimming pool barbecues, her sailing exploits, family and their activities, and her general practitioner husband and how they met in a hospital corridor. She told me he asked her out and she had to get permission from the matron. She also told me that her father was reluctant to let her train as a nurse and wanted her to keep working for him in his office. Jean was one to get what she wanted and was strong in her resolve.

Just like an old clock Jean was gradually winding down. There were days when she wanted to stay in bed, and there were days when she didn't want to eat or shower. She was sponged in bed and at times had brandy and dry ginger from her special little glass. Several days before she died, I assisted the nurse to take her to the toilet. I could smell stale feces and thought that she needed some help with this problem. However, Jean was not easy to advise and had rejected the aperient we had bought for her. In her weak physical state, the nurse and I changed her nightdress, gave her a warm sponge, and put her hands in the bowl. As I raised her right arm she strongly expressed pain. This happened again when we lifted her legs to soak her feet in the basin of water. It was not the time to consider bowel management, as there were more important soul and comfort matters to attend to.

The general practitioner had called the day before and Jean had said she didn't have any pain so, forgetting Jean's dementia, the general practitioner ceased her anti-inflammatory. She had also ordered blood and urine tests. It must have been difficult for the general practitioner to be in agreement with the nursing team, who strongly felt that Jean's dying was near, when the patient herself rose to the occasion of a doctor's visit. So many patients do so, as if it is encoded in their psyche to look good for the doctor. Fortunately a palliative care specialist was able to come to the home and to meet with all the family members. There was unified agreement that Jean's comfort and dignity were all important at this time. An order was given for baseline medication to be delivered by a syringe driver and for breakthrough medication to also be given as needed. The medication was for pain relief, sedation and relieving anxiety.

Jean was reassured at all times, and one of the assistants sat beside her on the bed and, in the mind's eye, took Jean on a sailing boat journey. Family was present and there was special time with Jean's son who shed many healthy tears. Memories flowed and support was given as much as possible. Some family members arrived whom I had not met and stories were told of their losses and how those losses shaped their lives. A beautiful nurse from India was requested for the night Jean died. She gave breakthrough medication when needed, sponged the body when needed, and prayed to her God. I'm sure Jean felt the love that is "God" in all religions.

Next morning death rattles became distressing for the family. An injection was given to dry up these secretions as well as more breakthrough medication. I lifted Jean with the help of her daughter onto her favorite side and gently the breathing stopped after three hours. At that time two daughters and a granddaughter were sitting with me. It was a sacred time. The atmosphere in the room was peaceful, something that was perhaps helped by the lavender essence in the electric burner. It was a good death. There was a touching funeral and it was a true celebration of Jean's life. She wanted a painted coffin and it was decorated with strewn flowers and butterflies—her favorite symbol!

CHAPTER FIFTEEN

Who Decides?

When I first met Patricia she was eighty-seven and had been in a cognitively impaired state from brain damage for seventeen years after being hit by a truck. For the past fifteen years she had been in a dementia ward in a nursing home. It had been a long and emotional journey for her husband and three children. Her first husband and father of the three children had died and Patricia married a retired general practitioner whose wife had also died. They had three very happy years together before the accident.

At the time of surgery to relieve pressure on the brain, the husband and children had been warned that this was a serious injury and Patricia may not survive. The goal of surgery at the time was difficult for the family to assess and as the son said, "We still had hope that she would get better." In that numbing time of shock and grief, clear guidance stating the benefits and burdens of treatment needs to be given to the family—preferably in a group—as different members of the family will have memories which may be based on what they wanted to hear at the time from their own perspective.

It is often too easy for a health professional to avoid giving adequate time and explanation in such a family meeting. This may be because they are unskilled at breaking bad news, they do not wish to be held accountable, or they have their own beliefs and values that may be at odds with what is in the best interest of the patient and family. It is ideal in such a situation for the family to have known and trusted friends for support as they consider what their mother would have wanted if she could have told them and what they can live with. Can they live with the fact that they are committing their mother to maybe live for many years in a moribund state of decline, having nurses feed, bath, and protect the body from bedsores? Can they live with the decision to cease treatment and never know what would have been achieved with rehabilitation?

In Patricia's case, everything had been done in the area of rehabilitation. Patricia attempted to talk but her words could largely not be understood. She had seizures, which seemed to make her more alert. One such seizure caused her to fall out of her chair and break her hip, which received surgery. The most distressing event for Patricia's children was the fact that abscesses formed under her teeth and the recommendation was that all her teeth should be removed. However, one daughter in particular felt that pain had to be present and suffered and her mother was unable to complain.

Patricia's room was furnished with a large board, which was covered with photographs of a productive and happy life. Her second husband, who visited her every day, died several years before she did and the situation became too distressing for at least one of her children. Another of the children lived overseas for many years and visited as often as possible but was limited by distance. Patricia's son remained loyal to the memory of his mother but again felt he had to consider his own family. Some of the staff of the nursing home where Patricia was cared for had known her for long periods of time and she responded to being fed whether by reflex or because hunger was a physical symptom she did feel.

The nursing home staff felt she had minimum pain and she was given regular mild pain relief. Her limbs became contracted. The family organized for a neuro physiotherapist to visit regularly and for a private caregiver to visit and read to her. Her radio was left on a classical channel, but in a ward where dementia patients were cared for, the noises of the other residents could be heard. The thought that their mother could have pain worried her children. It is difficult to lie in bed in one position and be moved for daily nursing care without pain and discomfort. Not knowing that their mother was where she wanted to be from a physical point of view also worried them, such as having no say or choice about enjoyment in life other than to open her mouth, and even in the little things like having control of a comfortable body temperature by requesting bedclothes on or bedclothes off.

Patricia was a woman who had so much more enjoyment than eating in her life before that accident. She was a churchgoer, a professional woman, a sportswoman, a mother, a grandmother, a wife, a traveler, and a valued friend. It was not difficult to have empathy for the family, and when I was asked to talk to them as a palliative care nurse about a palliative care approach, we began first to explore the South Australian Palliative Care Act of 1995. This was the same year that Patricia had her accident, yet so little seemed to be known about the contents of the act by all those involved in Patricia's care, apart from the right to refuse treatment, which was how the general practitioner was instructed in the case of a chest infection.

The act clearly states that life-sustaining measures do not need to be continued if there is no hope of recovery and if the patient is in a moribund or vegetative state. With this in mind, the family requested from their general practitioner a referral to a palliative care physician. The physician saw Patricia and at the family's request asked the staff to consider a palliative approach to food, such as giving food for pleasure rather than for sustaining life. The children remarked on their mother's sweet tooth and the staff agreed that she did enjoy her desserts and cordial. I suggested that giving a drink of water before food might be considered, as thirst rather than hunger may be the discomfort. This new idea and approach caused a stubborn divide in those supporting the family and those caring for Patricia in the dementia ward of the nursing home.

The palliative care physician could see both sides of the story, and the family and I sought to have a consultative meeting with the director of care of the nursing home and her colleagues. On a phone call to the director of care to thank her for her time, I was told, "We will have to run parallel on this one." How does that make the family feel? The atmosphere and exchange of energy was not one of non-judgmental, unconditional loving support. How could it be, without a common goal? Especially after the family could see with their own eyes the suffering on their mother's face when for brief moments consciousness seemed to return to her body and after video recording it on their phones.

As a palliative care nurse I am reassured if the person's wish is to make the body a comfortable enough place to live in while they prepare to die. Dying is a process and calls for much sensitivity and respect for the soul or essence of the person. For me it is not a body to be turned on or off as some euthanasia advocates may see dying. In Patricia's case, the family recalled their mother's values when a relative or friend had a debilitating stroke. They felt strongly that her wishes would not be to have her life prolonged, as at those times she had said, "If that ever happens to me, please shoot me!" With impaired thinking capacity, Patricia may not have had the judgment to keep her mouth closed and to gradually fade away from lack of food as so many nursing home patients do.

Knowing that there are those who have the ability to communicate with patients in a coma, I had asked a general practitioner I shared another patient with and who was a Reiki master if he or someone he recommended could visit Patricia and try to get a sense of her wishes. This was facilitated and a man of many years' experience in the area of energy medicine visited Patricia. This man, Jonathan, was also gifted in the art of dousing, when a response to a direct question can be intuited in a similar way to water divining. There are many scientific papers written about ways to connect with the breath of people in a coma. The work of Arnold and Amy Mindell comes to mind in the book *Coma: A Healing Journey* (1999).

When Jonathan was diagnosing Patricia's energy field, he obviously connected with her and she would smile, grimace, and try to talk. However, although there were family witnesses to Patricia's responses, they were dismissed as being "airy fairy" rather than thinking "outside the box" in our attempt to assist Patricia and her family in whatever way possible and available. It was Jonathan's opinion that there were times when the consciousness or energy body left Patricia's body and also returned. The question he asked when he performed his dousing ritual was, "Do you want to go or do you want to stay?" The answer he intuitively received was that Patricia wanted to go and in two months' time. Jonathan received a sense that a family member needed time to adjust and to feel that a palliative care approach was the correct action, given all the circumstances. The family was told by the palliative care physician that he would be able to look after Patricia in a private hospital where there were more trained staff members if it was the wish of the family. It was up to the family to make the decision.

The staff did pop in to check on Patricia regularly but mostly they saw an unresponsive person who, when the spoon touched her lips, opened her mouth and swallowed. They were not seeing what we were seeing which was a soul (or some consciousness) trapped in a body—a very impaired body with no hope of recovery. When the family requested the pain relieving syrup ordered by the palliative care physician be given as needed, there was a long wait, as it had to be given by a registered nurse and there was not always one available. Drops had also been ordered to be put on Patricia's tongue each evening for sedation and relief from anxiety and when she was distressed as needed. The family became more anxious and less confident that these medications were being given, as there was a difference in the judgment of pain and discomfort between the nursing home staff and the family and palliative care team. It was stated by the family at a meeting that it was their wish to give medication to be sure, rather than to be in doubt, as to their mother's comfort. Their good intentions were clear.

Just when a legal decision was to be made as to the most appropriate course of action, Patricia had a seizure and the general practitioner, on consulting the palliative care physician, commenced a continuous infusion of medications to relieve pain, sedate, and relax. Patricia slipped away peacefully two days later. The family had time by the bedside and a pastoral care person read the twenty-third Psalm and said prayers. There were pink roses by her bed and gentle attention from a palliative care nurse who cleansed and moisturized her mouth and smoothed her face and body with a perfumed lotion. It seemed so right and it was exactly two months, as predicted, from the time of Jonathan's visit.

CHAPTER SIXTEEN

The Animals Came
to Pay Homage

Arnold was in his late eighties and suffering from carcinoma of the abdomen when I was called to his hospital bed. His daughter and a family friend were present. I had been asked to introduce myself and to offer support for going home. During the first meeting the question of "Why me?" was voiced. Not knowing what Arnold's beliefs were, I mentioned that understanding the "god" factor was like an ant trying to understand the working of the New York stock exchange (source not remembered) and that often a person places their faith in nature and the laws of nature. I may have also said that love and fear are two switches that cannot both be on at the same time. Following this interaction I was left with the feeling that we had a tentative relationship forming. I spoke to Arnold's daughters outside the hospital room and they confirmed that he did not have a religious faith and that what I had said would have struck a chord with him.

I could sense that being in hospital gave Arnold a sense of security and hope. He spoke about the physiotherapist being available and of his wish to be able to walk around the bed before going home. Looking at his two edematous legs, I could see that this was an unrealistic hope.

I looked him in the eye and told him that each day he would wake up with so much energy and it was his choice as to how he spent that energy. He could spend it trying to walk around his bed and thoroughly exhaust his supply of energy or he could perhaps conserve his energy for more pleasurable and realistic goals such as reading his book and enjoying conversation with his family. I suggested that when he came home he could use a wheelchair to enjoy his veranda and he said he could accept this idea. His wife was also fearful of the responsibility of supporting this very ill man at home. In the hospital he was being fed intravenously and had a catheter and drain for the accumulated abdominal fluid. In an effort to get Arnold ready for home, the hospital staff decided to try him without the urinary drainage catheter, yet his medication included large doses of diuretic. At that stage he was not experiencing pain in his body.

The next day I visited Arnold to confirm the arrangements we had made after visiting his home. I found him experiencing painful spasms that were coming from his bladder area. He clutched my hand and said he was not able to think or talk about going home. I went to the nurses' station to seek relief for his discomfort, only to be told that he had to wait another ten minutes to see if the mild pain relief would work before being given the opioid that was ordered. This seemed like stupidity when the man was in so much agony. A machine determined that his bladder was indeed full and it was decided to reinsert the catheter, and he was given a small dose of opioid and three drops to sedate and calm him. Following this Arnold slept for four hours. On waking he felt so much better but instead of pursuing the arrangements for going home, the oncologist decided to keep Arnold in hospital for the weekend and give intravenous chemotherapy and an intravenous antibiotic even though infection had not been mentioned as a concern. In hindsight, this frightened and intelligent man had eight more days to live. Whose needs were being met—medical science's or the soul's needs?

The ambulance brought Arnold home on the Monday and placed him in the electric armchair that had been prepared for him. Knowing that this frail man would be in the chair all day long, a large foam square with a hole cut out to support his sacral area was placed under the patchwork quilt that his wife had made and which now covered the chair. I am aware of the concerns nursing staff have about using such aids as air cushions, but large foam squares that do not move are ideal for freeing the vulnerable sacral area from potential pressure and skin damage. The chair was placed opposite the French doors that opened on to the veranda, which overlooked a native reserve of gum trees and natural bushland. At his request, Arnold's wife moved the bird feeder and birdbath so that Arnold had a clear view of them.

Transfers from chair to bed were becoming increasingly more difficult for Arnold, as he was not able to carry his weight. We discussed help from sons-in-law and grandchildren, but this was not acceptable to Arnold's wife, who enjoyed her own space and privacy. Hiring a machine to stand transfer was also not possible. This resulted in Arnold spending more time in his own brass double bed. There is always significance in being in one's own bed. The bed replaced the chair opposite the French doors and pillows were placed so that Arnold could still see the bird feeder and birdbath. Colorful parrots came to visit and there were many bird sounds for Arnold to enjoy.

Arnold spent time with his wife and daughters reminiscing about the books he had written on the various chapters of his life. They proudly spoke about the steam train that he had made, the sailing that he had enjoyed, and his travels to the outback of Australia, where he discovered Aboriginal paintings and sacred sights. The dressing table in Arnold's room was covered with photographs, and in his last days and nights music gently filled the room along with the scent of lavender. Two palliative care assistants gently sponged Arnold in bed and his frequent cold drinks were lovingly supplied by his wife, who also made small portions of his favorite food.

Arnold asked me what would happen when he'd had enough. He was having pain-relieving medication subcutaneously twice a day. This was commenced with the bed to chair transfers. Drops to sedate and relieve anxiety were given prior to a rest and quiet time in the afternoon and for sleeping. In answer to his question I replied that as he grew weaker and couldn't change the position of his body, he would become more uncomfortable and we would give medication to relieve these discomforts. Also, if he wanted to have more sleepy times he could have medication for that, too. I reassured him that he was in charge and that we were there to support his requests. I talked about intuitive knowing and that he would know when it was time to say good-bye to his wife and family. As he had grandchildren, I told him about one grandson who had said his grandfather hadn't fallen off his perch—rather he stepped off it! I said this was a time to show leadership to his children, as facing death is just another of life's lessons to be learned.

The amazing thing about caring for Arnold in his final week was the amount of birds and animals that came to visit. Yes, there were the birds, but also a kangaroo hopped by this suburban home, and koalas sat in the tree next to the house and came into the courtyard. The first day home we saw two beautiful dogs with collars, both bounding with life and energy, cross the footpath and try desperately to enter Arnold's room. They had not been seen in the street before and no one knew where they had come from. The day Arnold died there was a koala with a baby on its back visiting.

Comparing this setting in nature with death in a hospital room raises many questions and highlights the comfort that can be obtained from acting according to an individual's values and what brings personal meaning. It also teaches the next generation about death, as what is seen and experienced goes a long way to removing fear. What is hidden in hospital environments does little to help educate those experiencing end of life decisions. To form trusting relationships and practice person-centered care is preferable to rescuing or trying to shield a person from suffering. Although birds have been known to peck at hospital windows, it could be difficult to have visits from a kangaroo and koalas.

CHAPTER SEVENTEEN

The Power of Fear

James was ninety-three when we were asked to assist with his care. He was forthright about dying at home and not going to a nursing home. Although Jane, his wife, was fifteen years younger, she was finding it a strain to maintain his clothes, meals, and being woken many times during the night when James got up to go to the toilet. He insisted on getting dressed in his tweed suit each day and on having a "proper" midday meal. He also enjoyed going out for meals with his sons. Jane was his second wife and was adored by this very intelligent man who had educated himself with scholarships to be a successful businessman.

James was the only sibling in his family to be born with the ability to hear and as such had played a significant role in the lives of his two brothers and sister. His mother had worked at sewing and cleaning to make sure the deaf children had special education. His father had been a trade unionist and as a result of a dispute had been demoted to a laboring job. Life could not have been easy for James, yet he talked about it with a smile and gestured with a "chin up" movement of his head. He was proud of his background and the pranks he and his brother had got up to. A younger brother had died of an illness and James told how he rode his bike to get the doctor but it was too late. This had been a significant event that was often retold in the times we shared. I would be kneeling massaging his feet and he would be sitting in his chair looking down at me. One day I said to him, "Your feet are cold. That means you have a warm heart." He replied, "I think you know that." Perhaps his younger brother's death was the underlying unconscious cause of James' death anxiety.

James was not an easy man to care for, as everything had to be done precisely and in a known and familiar way. He had early signs of dementia, irritable bowel, and a pacemaker for his heart condition. The doctor who did a home visit each month was frequently chastised for being late. On the subject of this doctor an enlightening story was told. One son had expressed the wish for the subject of spirituality to be introduced. The doctor referred to a book he had just read about Ernest Shackleton, the heroic Antarctic explorer. The doctor reported that in the book, Shackleton referred to God as "the third man" because when he and his party were in life threatening situations the "third man" would send the solution in a thought form.

James told us that he had lost his faith in religion and God at an early age when his intelligent brain sought rational answers. Maybe the death of his brother might also have been a contributing factor. He was quite happy to talk about the faith that had supported both his wives. His first wife was a Catholic and was comforted by her religion until her death, which he had witnessed. She had died quietly while sitting in her chair. His second wife had died in hospital. He had visited her to say good-bye in hospital and grieved for her for many months. This was demonstrated with tears and a heart wrenching, "I miss her." When driving past the church where they were married, he would remind us that Jane was buried there.

It would seem that James's experiences of death were not fearful yet, at the age of ninety-five, he was troubled by dreadful death anxiety at night. This required a considerable amount of medication and human warmth to alleviate. One son was particularly concerned about giving medication, as he believed this could contribute to a fall. Again, whose needs are we meeting? It was a difficult situation, as the sons had medical power of attorney and were never present overnight. James had twenty-four hour care, which was made as seamless as possible with nurse case coordination. Being an effective patient advocate is difficult and was very difficult as the care team strove to juggle orders from the family and James' wishes.

Our goal was comfort and patient-centered care. This attitude to end of life care seeks to honor the person's life and begs the question of "How do you want to be remembered?" James clearly wanted to be remembered as having control of his life and resisted being bossed. It was also difficult to avoid the triggers that set off angry and irrational outbursts. One of these triggers was money, which he liked to keep in his wallet. Another was the wheelchair, which he did not care to use. He did take to his walking stick and in his later years he accepted help with cleaning and dressing after visits to the toilet. Standing to shave was another matter. Another trigger was being asked questions. With the handicap of his brain not working as it once did, if answers did not come he felt foolish and became angry. James was a proud man and we became skilled at anticipation and framing what we needed to know in a way that left him thinking it was his idea.

I believe James's wife masked many of her physical symptoms for fear of burdensome treatment. She saw it as her duty to care for James and in the last months of her life forced herself to get up, shower, and follow the familiar routines when I believe she would have loved a day in bed. It was just not in her nature. How often what is important and life enriching to people like this couple is not considered or available in institutional care.

Food was a major pleasure for James. Jane was a good cook but was growing weak and frail. She needed help with meals and for the times when there was a mess from irritable bowel accidents. After Jane died, James would feel sad sitting at the table without her. To satisfy his love of eating out, every Sunday his sons alternated in taking him to either a fish restaurant or to a hotel that served Sunday lunch in a style that reminded him of life in England. There he was, bent over his walking stick, dressed in his tweed suit and welcoming the greetings from restaurant staff that remembered that he had a glass of red wine with his meal. A favorite choice was oysters and there was a story to tell about how he came to be fond of oysters as a boy. James would also recall the time he was sick after eating oysters on a trip to Ireland. His notes contained suggestions from his sons regarding his menus. At this time of life food is mostly for the soul; it is about remembering associations and acts of loving concern. One son went to three butcher shops before finding tripe, which was a dish James's mother cooked. A glass of sherry was served before lunch and a glass of red wine after lunch when he was back in his chair.

James's daily routines continued until the pacemaker began to fail and nights became a torment of anxiety. The family found it difficult to come to terms with our night reports, as the man they experienced in the daytime was a different man to the man who was up and down in the night, demanding this and that in a futile attempt to allay his fear. We quickly found that human warmth complemented medication. He liked to have a presence near him, stroking an arm or leg and giving reassurance. Not all his caregivers had the gift of giving a mother's love, which is what Mother Mary Potter of the Little Company of Mary recommended. She wanted to serve the dying like the mother of Jesus at the foot of the cross. Too many times end of life is about medicine and the concern is about the benefits and burdens of medications. Simple things like soft music, loving touch, kind words, inspiring verse, and a calm presence are overlooked in the rush to get things done.

With James, standing became difficult and it is often this realization that the body isn't working that brings home the reality that death is near. James looked me in the eye at this stage and said, "I'm in trouble, aren't I?" I didn't try to talk to him in a hopeful way. I confirmed what he had just said and reassured him that he was in good hands and that perhaps he would soon see his younger brother he had tried to save by making every effort to get the doctor to come. I agree with the twelve principles of palliative care. The first principle states that patients have the right to know when they are dying and what to expect (The Age Health and Care Study Group, UK, 1999).

Sleep is so important and is a break from suffering. In this case it was difficult to obtain adequate medication orders. A palliative care approach would say that "pain is what the patient says hurts." It is not so much about pharmacology and recommended doses but what the patient is experiencing. We know in cancer pain that medication is increased to whatever level is required to give relief without concern. In James's case it was existential pain and angst, but some members of the family expressed the fear that if more anti-anxiety medication was given, respiration would be depressed and such a death would be euthanasia.

This highlights the need to understand the principle of double effect. What is the intention of giving the medication? Is it to relieve suffering or is it given to hasten death? Then there are the projected feelings of the family members and when people are in an emotional state logic and objectivity are hampered. These are all-important questions and need explanations if possible. I likened the situation to childbirth and the need for medical intervention to ensure best outcomes for mother and baby. In this case it is to ensure that death is timely and supported.

The aim (with reference to the World Health Organization's definition of palliative care) is neither to hasten nor postpone death. It begs the question of how much control do health professionals really have? Those who work with dying people have many stories about the patient dying when they are ready and in spite of medication it would seem.

There is no universally correct response to patient and family discomfort. Much will depend on what are the expectations and hopes of those affected. Appropriate intervention may take many forms, often being tentative or exploratory. —Emeritus Professor Ian Maddocks

For all the caring team to be on the same page was a difficult process for James and his family, as everyone had their own view of the way forward. One way of solving this problem was to invite his sons to assist with care. This was necessary from time to time, as transfers required more than one person and particularly so if there had been an unexpected bowel action. The word "dignity" is often used when death is mentioned. What is dignified for one person may not be dignified for another. It became more and more difficult to respect this gentleman's wishes, as he still expressed the desire to go for a walk, to get up, and sit in his chair—even when his body became extremely weak and he had difficulty making his legs follow his wishes. He would have good periods and this seemed to depend on his heart's performance without the assistance of his pacemaker. Again nature seems to be our best teacher. So often medications are blamed for sleepiness when it is just the body needing to rest. In this case it was more important to observe the effects of medication, whether it was medication for bowel management or death anxiety, than to be overly concerned with the dose. To give non-judgmental, loving care requires shutting down the need for control and being right, and just being in the moment.

This was the beginning of a peaceful, terminal phase for a man who had achieved and witnessed much in his lifetime. In spite of the medication, the family was able to see that fear broke through the regime of medications. He clutched offered hands tightly and was very distressed in spite of soft voices reminiscing about past events in his life. I put my cheek up against his cheek and encouraged him to just concentrate on his breathing and know that he was a good man who had always tried his best. The murmuring continued. I continued. Now it is time to let go of this life and to just lie on a grassy slope and watch the clouds drift over the sun while you breathe more slowly, with the knowledge in your heart that you are loved and will be remembered by many … living on through your genes and in people's memory … no fear … just love …

Medication was given more frequently until a peaceful state existed with easier breathing. This was the time when family members performed at their best. The bedside vigils became more peaceful and less stressful. Stepchildren came to visit and to honor the man who had made their mother happy and secure for some fifteen years. Tension made way for common love and concern. Lavender perfume filled the room, which became sacred space. James had a favorite palliative care assistant who could get him to do things outside his routine, such as taking him for a drive, cutting his hair, and generally calling him Jamie when his general title of address was "mister." It seemed fitting that James chose to die when this assistant was giving him his final wash and position change. She spoke gently when she put his false teeth in place, and while it seemed impossible from a physical point of view, he cooperated with this procedure and peacefully died several hours later with his children present. In the end it was a good death, but as in the Christian message there was much suffering and angst before death united all the health professionals and family members in the common wish for comfort—in all areas of James's life.

CHAPTER EIGHTEEN

Natural Instinct

A young mother was dying of breast cancer. I will name her Elizabeth. She had a father who was a doctor, and her husband ran a small business. The children were both under five when their mother died. Elizabeth's mother and their father had cared for them. Elizabeth had sent her husband away from their home to live elsewhere while she made every effort to fight the cancer, which was dominating her life. She needed time alone as well as time in her roles of mother and wife.

I remember her request for an electric wheelchair so she could sit viewing her garden and watching the birds. The husband of a previous patient of mine had bought an electric wheelchair for his wife's last days, and on learning of Elizabeth's need he readily paid for this chair to be delivered to her. Kindness in many forms is seen in times of illness and death. The notion of community rather than individualism gives expression to these acts of generosity.

When Elizabeth was dying, her parents, husband, and children were present, and I was witness to one of my most profound lessons. After her last breath, the father of her two young children lifted them onto the bed and let them see that their mother wasn't breathing anymore. He asked the children to help him take off her wedding ring so that they would have it to remind them of her. I have never seen a medical text recommend such a beautiful act. At the time it seemed the right thing to do.

Last acts such as washing the body of the person who has died are very much part of the grieving process. Many sons and daughters have thanked me for letting them help in this process. Often it is a necessity because of the weight of the person who has died. Many have said that it was a treasured privilege to choose the clothes to be worn and that it helped to bring the death into reality by helping with washing, dressing, and changing bedclothes. Chairs can be placed at the bedside for those who wish to sit in remembrance or prayer. I like to leave the hands above the bedclothes in a natural pose. Many loved ones choose to hold a hand. This also seems to help confirm the reality of the death.

I remember a nun in Singapore speaking about how she cared for those in her care. If a person in her care was dying, she would make sure the patient and family were served tea or refreshments from the very best china. The end of a life is indeed a special time. The busy activities that dominate everyday life are put on hold for a period and personal values and beliefs are tested for their usefulness. How often does a person hold on to habits and thoughts that no longer serve in a useful way to their personal growth? Death is a great teacher in so many ways. Elisabeth Kubler-Ross, the Swiss psychiatrist who taught the world so much about death and dying, writes that all fears have their roots in the fear of death and by conquering this fear a person conquers all the small fears of life, and that to learn to die is to learn to live.

It has also been said that when parents die courageously, children will have the courage to live. I often wonder about the lives of Elizabeth's two children, as it is many years since they removed their mother's wedding ring.

CHAPTER NINETEEN

Who Will Be There?

Peter was in his sixties and had been diagnosed with lung cancer, prostate cancer, emphysema, and a gut disorder. He was an intelligent, principled man who had studied philosophy at a university. He was born into a family in England who saw duty to one's country as a noble act. It was expected that Peter would find a career in the army, and he did for a time. It was this army experience that perhaps gave him "a ladder" to enter the next world.

I had been asked to visit Peter initially by an email, which asked how best to support him, as he was currently a pensioner. NurseLink Foundation is a charity and the supportive care given to Peter was pro bono. Our care demonstrated, in the most poignant way, how the rewards for supporting a dying person who has chosen to die consciously can be truly inspiring and something that money cannot buy.

For eight weeks I visited Peter. On the first visit we covered an enormous amount of territory. The conversation began with a history of his medical and hospital journey. He had been in and out of a large public hospital, had accepted the treatments offered, and had told his story to one specialist after another. Now he knew his time had come to make the final journey and he wanted to be in charge of it. He wanted to do it his way and in his time. Meditation had been a key factor in his warding off the cancers and ill health. His mind was strong and his determined wish was that he would die mindfully.

The first visit progressed to exploring Peter's beliefs and life philosophy and I was amazed at how our paths into the mysteries of this life and the next had taken similar pathways. He strongly believed in a life after death and that the energy that leaves the body at the time of death carries the soul imprint to another existence. This may have been a factor in the strong bond that formed between this remarkable man and his very good friend Julie in whose house he had chosen to die. He found comfort in the fact that he could feel the presence of his grandmother, Nora, when he looked at me.

On my second visit he told me that he had been searching "the arsehole of Mexico for Nembutal" via the Internet. I suggested he might like to try what palliative care had to offer and that he obtain a referral to a palliative care specialist doctor. His general practitioner was pleased to do this, as he had experienced this doctor's teaching at the university and felt more comfortable with this approach rather than what Peter had suggested earlier when he visited him and stated that he wanted to die.

A home visit by the palliative care doctor occurred and the assessment was that Peter wasn't sure if he wanted to live or die, but a trusting relationship had formed. For the next few weeks Peter put immediate dying on hold and consideration was given to his bowel management, nutrition (including supplements), getting enough sleep and rest, writing his diary, and attending to the legal aspects of making a will and formulating an advance care directive. During this time, Peter's special friend was becoming more and more involved in the struggle, the analysis of the process, actioning requests for visits from supportive friends, and generally tying up earthly concerns.

Peter was passionate about their garden and was committed to organic gardening. Here was a man of no religious adherence feeling connected to nature, the universe, universal energy, and the bigger picture in a way that I found uncanny. The atmosphere in the home was one of profound peace. Peter accepted a visit from NurseLink Foundation's physiotherapist and energy therapist. The physiotherapist projected a vital, sunny energy and this together with postural drainage resulted in a helpful clearing of mucus from Peter's lungs. His attempts to achieve a similar result with nebulized medications, oxygen, and coughing had formerly caused him to vomit. Vomiting into a practical plastic bucket was just one of the discomforts Peter had endured. His intake of nutritious food and drink was decreasing rapidly with evident weight loss. Later, when Peter died and I washed his skin and bone frame with as much tenderness as I could muster, I was shocked to see the state of his body, which had been largely hidden by clothing.

Peter's mind never faulted in its clarity and he warmly welcomed the energy therapist for sessions of attunement. Attunement is a form of energy medicine originally developed by Lloyd Arthur Meeker and his colleagues (1907-1954) and was taught as a central feature of personal spiritual practice. Like Qigong, Reiki, and Therapeutic Touch, attunement is a healing modality offered through the hands. It is recognized as a complementary therapy, as it lacks published scientific research.

Peter said he gained benefit from a chakra clearing meditation in which I introduced the colors and concepts of chakras that I had learned from the medical intuitive and author, Caroline Myss. For this process, Peter sat with a calm mind and closed eyes to facilitate an inner process. I began with the color red, which represents the base chakra (located at the base of the spine) and is a metaphor for the family into which we are born. Peter was encouraged to breathe in the color red and reflect on the people who had shaped his early beliefs, habits, and behavior.

Orange was the next color to breathe in and while Peter was mindfully breathing in orange, I was clearing the sexual chakra (located above the pubic bone). I reminded him that this chakra was associated with a person's sexuality, relationships, power, productivity, and money. Forgiveness and release were suggested before inviting Peter to breathe in the color yellow. This is the color associated with the solar plexus chakra (located near the naval) and represents self-esteem and personhood. As I made hand movements to clear this chakra, Peter was encouraged to reflect on his achievements and struggles to be comfortable with himself.

Green is the color of the heart chakra and here Peter was encouraged to reflect on the unselfish love and joys of his life as he breathed in the color green and saw in his mind's eye the color fill his body from his crown to his feet and out into the earth. Blue was the next color to bring to mind and Peter was told that it represented the throat chakra, which is our source of communication and will. At this point in the meditation, the suggestion for Peter to think of things he still had to say as he proceeded toward closure of this lifetime. Maybe there were things said in the past that needed to be amended in some way.

The final major chakras are the forehead chakra and the crown chakra. The forehead chakra is indigo and is in the region of our third eye, which assists in developing insight and seeing the larger picture. The crown chakra, with the color violet, is a central chakra dealing with consciousness and spirituality. Peter was encouraged to see his essence, the embodiment of all his actions and reactions, trials, and successes, as a pearl which would rise on every breath in a tube connecting the heart chakra with the crown chakra. He was encouraged to picture the crown chakra opening like a lotus flower and to breathe in the color violet knowing that when the time was right his Higher Power would harvest his pearl. As I left, Peter said, "That was lovely!"

I was introduced to Therapeutic Touch when I became a member of the U.S. Nurse Healers Association and experienced at first hand the work of both Dora Kunz, who was born with clairvoyant faculties, and Dolores Kreiger, PhD RN, the recognized founders of Therapeutic Touch. This complementary therapy is the most recognized technique used by practitioners of holistic nursing. I am also a qualified Reiki practitioner and have recently been awarded a diploma in clinical hypnosis. It is difficult to discern where these modalities overlap, and I strive to be guided by intuition and to always have the intention to be a loving conduit for these energies. Therapeutic Touch practitioner Janet Macrae, in her book titled *Therapeutic Touch – A Practical Guide* (1988), has this to say:

"The practice of Therapeutic Touch involves the use of oneself (that is, one's own localized energy field) as an instrument to help rebalance areas within the patient's field that have become obstructed and disordered by disease. As a relaxed, 'totally present' state of being is required to do this, the practitioner has to have some control over thoughts and emotions as well as physical gestures. The use of conscious intent (sometimes called intentionality) is thus essential for the practice of Therapeutic Touch. The practitioner must establish the intent to become a calm, focused conduit for the universal life energy and to direct that energy to the patient."

Back to Peter. The palliative care doctor had ordered pain-relieving medication in the form of a slow release opioid and an opioid syrup for breakthrough or incident pain. Medication of four sedating drops helped Peter to sleep and rest. What was most important for him was to be in charge and to work doses out for himself. In the last two weeks of life, he ate a little of what he fancied and sipped on a supplement drink. Bowel care was tried but because of Peter's diseased gut he was hesitant to take aperients. Weight loss continued in a dramatic fashion. He insisted, however, that he still had ends to tie up and his mind was clear.

The day before Peter died, he requested a visit from a music therapist.

Special soul connecting live music was strummed on a guitar and could only be described as a facilitated meditation. For an hour Julie and I, from our position in the kitchen, could hear and feel the effect of this intuitive playing. More importantly, Peter found the experience to be of benefit and asked if the therapist could come again the next day. This was the day Peter died and it was as though he knew it was to be his important day and was assembling his team who would support the process of his dying.

Under the guidance of the palliative care physician, a subcutaneous continuous infusion was commenced the night before Peter died. He was very calm as he accepted this form of medication to make him comfortable and to keep death anxiety and nausea at bay, as well as control troublesome secretions building up in his throat, commonly called death rattles. For the first time I saw Peter's bedroom—he had never been a traditional patient. His days were spent on a couch in a room dressed with books, CDs, and the most beautiful woodcarvings that he had crafted. There was a collection of hats on top of the bookcase—all had significance. Perhaps most telling of all was that he had his cats in attendance. How can one describe the comfort they gave? There were also regular deliveries of fresh flowers to lift the spirits of both the patient and Julie, the guardian or keeper of the promise.

In spite of his intellectual acceptance of death, Peter found it hard to die. He had said his good-byes. He felt comfortable that his emotional and spiritual house was in order. He had written to his father who was still alive in England. He had written all he felt he needed to write in his diary. He had the uncompromising support of his special and loyal friend, Julie. He had chosen the music he wanted to have playing while his breath failed. It was to be Paul Horn playing the flute in the sacred site of the Great Pyramid. It was raining, and he felt his garden's needs were being met. He said the rain was a good sign. He had medication to keep his body comfortable while he made these preparations.

As Peter settled comfortably in his double bed, I knelt by his bed to be at eye level and asked him if he could remember an achievement that took courage and bravery. He told me he had learned to parachute when he was in the army. I felt I could now plan a session of hypnosis to assist the imminent transition. As I had previously introduced the rainbow and had heard him confirm that he "saw" colors in his dreams, I used the rainbow for the induction into a trance state. I invited him to walk across a lush meadow and to climb on board the special white plane that was waiting for him.

Once he was on board the plane soared, climbing steadily to the required height for parachuting. Peter was instructed to put on his parachute and test it. He nodded that he felt confident with the parachute, as he had packed it himself. I asked him to take the leap to earth and to see his body parachuting to earth but not to be concerned, as what he saw was only his old body which was no longer required. In the cockpit was his higher self piloting the special white plane to another existence, or, as Florence Nightingale writes, the soul entering the arch of triumph to live again in a freer atmosphere.

There was peace in the room and I left Peter in Julie's care. I returned in the early afternoon, the time arranged with the music therapist. For three hours the room was filled with a medley of musical notes played with intuition as the conductor. Peter's pulse was faint and rapid, yet it continued. Julie stroked his head and whispered encouragement. A vase of red roses was by the bed. Yet Peter stayed. The music therapist left and the CD of Paul Horn playing *Inside The Great Pyramid*—with themes of fulfillment, resurrection, initiation, enlightenment, and eternity—again filled the room. This time Peter took his last breath in time with the end of the concert. Julie said, "That is as good as it gets!"

CHAPTER TWENTY

An Unsupported Death—Barbara

This story was told to me by a young anesthetist during a round of golf. We had not met before and my fellow player had asked me about my working life. On hearing that I was a palliative care nurse, she told me the story of her mother's death. It was a heart-wrenching story, as the daughter was an only child. Her father had died many years ago. She recalled that her mother, Barbara, had lived a full and productive life as a photographer. She had given her only child the best education, and her daughter had desired to make her mother proud of what she had achieved in her professional career as a result of her many sacrifices.

Yet in her time of greatest need, Barbara had not confided her intention of ending her life with her daughter. Maybe this was viewed as a way of sparing her daughter. It was the act of a woman who wished to be in control of her dying and who did not want anyone to take the blame for the action she took to end her life. A noble thought, but the actions of her mother had left a deep and lasting wound, which the daughter felt she would carry for life. As an anesthetist, the daughter was familiar with the medications used in palliative care which would have eased her mother's dying and would have allowed her to hold and envelope her mother in love as she slipped into an unconscious state and the process of a supported death.

It was a shock for the daughter to be called to identify her mother's lifeless body. She had been at work and unaware of her mother's intentions when she discharged herself from the hospice. The memory was still haunting her. I do not remember much about our game of golf, as we were both in another place and time. The daughter was sharing her pain, and I was trying to put myself in her shoes and struggling with words of comfort. Hopefully much of our anger and frustration was released in the striking of golf balls. As health professionals we could see that a paternalistic approach that frequently refers the patient from one health specialist to another does not meet the end of life needs of all personalities. End of life is a time for deep sharing in a trusting environment. The quality of the empathetic relationship is as important as qualifications.

What the daughter found was Barbara's dead body half on and half off the bed. She had a pink plastic bag over her head and this molded to her face like a tight glove with all the air taken out of it. Tablets were strewn on the floor. There was a note of good-bye, which only added to the daughter's frustration and regret. This was all so very painful and was still raw even after the interval of several years. The daughter felt that she had let down this beautiful soul by not listening well enough to her wish to die in her own time.

For many years I have had the privilege to work alongside Ian Maddocks, who was appointed to the first chair in palliative care in the world at Flinders University, South Australia in 1986. As an educator and practitioner, he epitomizes all the qualities of a palliative care doctor. He balances left and right brain activities. In his words, the left hemisphere of the brain writes progress notes, prescribes doses, and orders tests, while the right hemisphere reaches out to the person and sits, waits, listens, and touches. He gives his phone number to all patients, nurses, and families for times of need. He sees the patient at home if that is where they choose to be.

When considering Barbara's end of life there were so many questions of why and why that way when there was good access to professional medical help. Barbara had been diagnosed with cancer; she had followed all the treatments offered and had spent time in a hospice. This was doing it by the book but it was not what supported this individual soul. All cultures have their own ways of viewing and supporting death. According to many religions, the lived life is the best preparation for death. In my view, death is an individual and lonely journey that needs a comfortable body and an atmosphere of peace and serenity.

With all the advances in pharmacology and modern technology, it seems odd that death outside the circles of recognized palliative care and hospice settings is not made more comfortable. Who "owns" death and who has the final say in how a person dies? To my mind it is the person, and health professionals play a supporting role, as do religions and the cultural beliefs of the family (in the broadest sense). When Dr. James Young Simpson first introduced chloroform in childbirth in 1893, there was an anti-religious myth in circulation that most churchmen, on biblical grounds, resisted the use of chloroform in childbirth. This myth seemed to especially disturb people who were poorly educated. The notion that the Catholic church is against medications being given to relieve pain and suffering, even if they cause death, is also a myth.

Physical pain is so much easier to accept and treat than existential pain. The cycle of birth and death is just that—a cycle with much meaning-making happening in between for the individual coming from a personal spiritual practice—whatever that spiritual practice may be. For many it is an organized religion; for others it may follow along the lines of Eastern traditions, which view life as a continuum of birth and rebirth. Many health professionals fear a "slippery slope" when death may become too easy to facilitate or may be influenced by others who have their own interests at heart rather than the person's whose death is expected. What kind of death, if we have a choice, do we want? The next chapter describes a "supported death."

CHAPTER TWENTY-ONE

A Supported Death

One day I received a phone call inviting me to afternoon tea. The call was from a lady, whom I will call Lady M, whose husband had made a considerable contribution to Australian society. When I met Lady M, her husband had died and she was living alone in a stately home surrounded by the most beautiful garden bordered by tall pine trees. We had tea and Lady M said the purpose of the visit was to put in place arrangements for her time of death and she wanted to be registered with my practice so that she knew she had nursing support when the time came. This was five years before her actual death at the age of ninety-one.

Looking back, Lady M was well before her time. This is the conversation I recommend for everyone. The tool to aid such a conversation is formalized into a document called an Advance Care Directive. "So sensible" was how Lady M described our conversation. I reassured her that she could stay at home among her lovely trees if that was her wish. She said she could imagine herself after death up there in the trees. How bravely this elegant woman spoke of the taboo subject of death and dying. We shared beliefs about life after death in the same natural way as eating the shortbread biscuits and drinking our tea.

The nurse/patient relationship grew over the years. One Christmas

I took her a jar of my homemade mayonnaise and she gave me a punnet of fresh raspberries. Another day I found her on her electric gopher, putting pansies in the holes the gardener had dug in the garden bed. She was happy and loving life, which I told her was the secret of a good death—to die with a love of life rather than a "poor me" attitude. She was as independent and self-reliant as she could be. I remember her innovative habit of clipping a peg onto the gas bottle that was in use to distinguish it from the one that was empty. Her house was full of the most beautiful furniture and paintings. She was so proud of the studio her husband had set aside for her so that she could work on her well-respected flower paintings. In this environment Lady M gently died.

The end began when she discharged herself from hospital where she had been admitted for pneumonia. She said she hated the narrow bed and cold sheets and missed her tortoiseshell cat. The cat also missed her and, when she came home her cat would hide under her dressing table and scrutinize all visitors with a growl. While Lady M maintained her daily bath with the assistance of a nurse, her world narrowed to her bedroom and bathroom. One exception was the day Princess Mary married Prince Frederik of Denmark when she made the valiant effort to watch the wedding on the television in the sitting room. She was by nature and experience very at home with royalty and all things regal.

The general practitioner she had chosen because she would do home visits and also because she had formed a trusting relationship with her visited, and together with the nurse a bedside meeting took place. To complement this team her daughter came to stay and to cook the most appropriate food, which in my view is about what nourishes the soul. It may be food loved as a child or food that is a reminder of a significant event. Most important is the love that goes into the preparation and the sharing of the food. Also important was that Lady M was made to feel in charge of this part of her life. She gave instruction to her financial advisor for funds to be available for her care and she watched her daughter sew the most beautiful white velvet pall for her coffin and complete a book about her father.

Covering the casket with a pall is a way to make a statement about the person who has died. It may have religious significance or it may be the flag of the person's country of citizenship. The pall, an ancient custom, is also a symbol of what was important to the person who has died. For some, the color white serves as a reminder of the white baptismal garment. All who were supporting this brave woman at this time felt the love that went into the sewing of the pall for Lady M by her daughter. This is a custom that is uncommon in today's environment of outsourcing death to others, be they hospitals, nursing homes, or funeral homes. The expression of grief takes many forms, from rage to living in the moment or to sewing the hem of a pall. Action and thoughts went hand in hand for Lady M's daughter.

I was not able to attend Lady M's funeral, so I do not know if other symbols were placed on the pall-covered casket. There may have been a photo. I later heard that the flowers, which were so much a part of her life, were a circle of red roses with dark green leaves. I do know that when I was making preparations for the time after breath had ceased, I was instructed by my patient to look in the wardrobe, where there was a special nightdress and negligee chosen for that time. How forward thinking and how considerate of her daughter, who when enveloped with emotion didn't need to attend to such questions as to what clothes to put on her mother after the nurse had respectfully washed her body and removed all nursing aids.

As is a frequent occurrence, not all people were comfortable supporting Lady M in the way of those immediately involved. The housekeeper felt that more could have been done from a medical point of view. To feel confident that the care was indeed the most appropriate, the general practitioner referred Lady M to a palliative care specialist. This specialist also made home visits, which is an ideal situation and the easiest way to see things from the patient's perspective. People are not themselves in a hospital bed surrounded by people who do not know or appreciate their personal history. To visit at home where we could hear the birds in the trees and be told by the owner of the house the story of the tree with a deformity and the one with a strange cry surely is to gain a psycho-spiritual connection not available in an institutional setting.

I remember visiting Lady M after the Royal Danish wedding. She was back in bed and had her eyes closed. Yet when I silently touched her brow she said, "Oh, Joy!" I said in a quiet voice, "Now you have your image. You are Mary and you are in a church filled with roses. You look radiant and beautiful and everyone loves you. You are walking down the aisle to meet your destiny." The reply came, "I hope the aisle is not too long!" What a privilege to have the opportunity to experience an event so profound.

CHAPTER TWENTY-TWO

The Journey Continued

I would describe Michael as an English gentleman. He had been an antique dealer and was married to a woman who had taught English at a private girls' school. He called her his "brown sugar." To my questioning gaze he added, "She is sweet but needs a little refinement!" They were both in their eighties and clearly very much in love. Michael was suffering from cancer but was refusing to have further treatment—even palliative radiation for a lesion in his neck that was painful and may have been helped by such treatment. His home was his sanctuary and he felt secure in the small front room of the house he shared with his wife.

For many weeks he had a night nurse, whom I would relieve in the morning. Michael called me "Joy who cometh in the morning." When I first met him, I had recently returned from attending a hospice conference in India and time spent in the Himalayas. I shared with Michael that while watching the sunrise over the Himalayas, I felt I was on top of the world and one with all. He looked me in the eye and said that he was secure in his "Catholic Anglican" faith and not interested in the Eastern wisdom I had discovered. So beliefs and life values were established in a bonding way.

One day the priest came to give him communion. For this he was dressed in his church robes and included Michael's wife in the ritual.

The comfort that ritual gave was visible. His daughter shared that the image of being a feather on the breath of God was one that her father found comforting. Care continued until one day when I was giving Micahel a massage and taking him through the colors of the rainbow. I related them to images such as the red berries in the front garden, the blue sky, the orange sun, the green foliage, and dark blue and violet flowers. Then I introduced the image of the feather on the breath of God and asked Michael if he felt like a feather in a gentle breeze. I noticed his actual breathing became very shallow and irregular. I felt like a midwife of the soul. His wife was in the room holding his hand and the whole room was filled with peace and calm.

This was broken when Michael opened his eyes and said, "I can't do it, Joy. I'll have a cup of tea!" We all laughed and I offered him porridge, too. He had been practising conscious dying in a moment that could be called sacred. I left and returned later in the day to have his wife tell me that Michael had described being knee-deep in water, seeing the glory of God and wanting to summon his whole family to give them a blessing. This was facilitated. Dying was being shared with those he loved.

When Michael did die, one grandson remarked, "My grandfather didn't fall off his perch. He stepped off!"

Of course there were the practical concerns of helping Michael's wife come to terms with his death and life without him. Our palliative care assistants cleaned the fridge, assisted with food preparation, and helped generally with caring for the house that was full of memories. It was impossible not to admire the collection of books on the bookshelf. These became a bond in the grieving period. I would share books that I was reading and vice versa. She and I attended movies and she worried that I might think that she was too old for a friendship. I admired her weaving skills, which became the focus for philosophical talks. She corrected my grammar when I gave her some of my writing to edit.

Support in the bereavement period is part of the hospice philosophy and takes many forms. In many ways Michael's wife and I became each other's wounded healer, as it was also a difficult time for me because I was experiencing the breakup of a thirty-year marriage. She sensed my need for the company of a safe, wise person. It was often on a Sunday evening that we met to share a movie or recordings of talks by the mythologist Joseph Campbell. I would receive inspiring verse written in a card by post. Eventually this wonderful woman coped with living by herself with family support and I became busy with the concerns of running a nurse practice and a career that took me to Malaysia. It was many years later that I received a call from her daughter to say that she had been admitted to a nursing home. I visited just before she died and although rather forgetful, she asked why I had come. I'm sure she felt that I was a messenger sent by her adored husband.

CHAPTER TWENTY-THREE

On the Subject of Soul

Peggy was an educated, elegant woman and the mother of three children. Her husband was successful in business and also known for his military career. Peggy played the roles of wife and mother as a woman in her position was expected to, according to the times. She had thought about the event of death and had signed a legal document called The Natural Death Act in South Australia. This act enables a person to refuse artificial prolongation of the dying process. When she had a severe stroke at the age of eighty-nine and was in a life-threatening situation, the hospital medical team kept Peggy alive by feeding her via a nasogastric tube into her stomach. This is not the natural provision of food and fluid. However, Peggy was not able to communicate with her medical team due to the stroke and her family were in shock and not sufficiently confident or informed to speak up on her behalf. In my experience this is very common. Tension arises between showing love and concern on the one hand, and on the other hand not feeling in a position to question the advice being given by the medical team for the concern that their feelings for their mother may be misinterpreted. Many, many times I have said in instances like this that love is "letting go."

What followed for Peggy was two years of living hell as she slowly declined and had extreme difficulty making her wishes known to the family and to the nursing home where she was being cared for by the best practice of the day. It is evident from Peggy's experience that the attitudes in nursing homes need to change. Her cries, almost constant, fell largely on deaf ears. She tried to fling herself over the bed rails on a number of occasions. Instead of trying to understand the reason behind this behavior, the nursing home staff put a mattress on the floor to soften her fall. Peggy was known in the nursing home as a patient who was a screamer who kept up a sound of repetitive "er ... er ... mumble, mumble"—with varying pitch and tone.

Peggy's body language demonstrated a frowning brow and pleading eyes. Her body became frailer and contracted. Her spine, which had given her trouble before the stroke, curved towards the fetal position. There were moments when her husband visited her and fed her that must have given her a reprieve from mental anguish. Her children felt they could visit more frequently after their father's sudden death, as he had demonstrated that his wife was his concern and responsibility. The children buried their father with a well-attended public funeral and in their grief moved toward their mother, who had always been there for them as children. At times she had been called on to explain or soften her husband's harsh discipline. This emotional turmoil for the children only worsened as they witnessed their mother's suffering and felt the burden of responsibility for its continuation.

Peggy's son, who is a musician, played his Hawaiian guitar to his mother on his visits. One daughter kept a video of her mother's decline and gave as much comfort as possible although she lived interstate. The other daughter who lived locally was more proactive and began to question the medication being given to her mother. She visited her mother's doctors and questioned why orders that had been given "as needed" were indeed seldom given. When I was asked to meet Peggy,

I arrived early and had no trouble finding her, as I could hear her cries and moans as I walked down the corridor toward her room.

I was greeted with a face lined with desperate pleas. I placed both hands on her cheeks and kissed her forehead and told her that her children had asked me to visit to help her. She stopped crying out and when the daughters found us together, we included Peggy as we talked about how to make her more comfortable. The nurse in charge was helpful in telling me about her pain relief and other medications. A lifter was being used to move Peggy onto a shower chair or into a chair in front of the TV along with other residents. Thickened fluids were being given, which Peggy indicated she did not like. She did like chocolate and the family lovingly gave this to her. In many ways it seemed that Peggy was just another body to shower, feed, mop up urine and feces for, and dress and sit in a chair.

The more I got to know Peggy's story, I realized that she was so much more than this. There was a soul trapped in her body and like a butterfly struggling to leave its chrysalis behind, Peggy wanted to leave this earthly experience. Her daughter who lived interstate reflected on her mother's beliefs and values before the stroke and wrote, "She seemed quite optimistic and told me that she was ready for the next big adventure in her life—her death. She told me that she believed she had done what she had come to do in this life and the next chapter was her death, and she was truly looking forward to it with some excitement. We talked about where she would like her ashes scattered and made a date to go and have a picnic there together so that I would know the exact spot, and we could celebrate the next phase of her life in this way."

I asked Peggy the question of her readiness to die and her eyes spoke. Her daughters had tears in their eyes, too. It was one of those moments of profound connection. I was asked if I would care for Peggy in her unit, which was still in the family. I agreed. Following the weekend an ambulance was ordered to transport Peggy back to an environment where she could feel herself—in spirit at least. The family was relieved to discover that I could offer Peggy twenty-four hour nursing in her own home with a palliative care physician in charge.

I was asked to take Peggy home for whatever time was needed to give Peggy comfort in all areas of her life, not just in the physical but also care in an environment that provided memories and gave her a sense of herself and the role she had played as a wife, mother, health professional, hostess, and so much more. From the moment of leaving the nursing home, there was no more calling out; there was just supportive, loving care with appropriate medication, which relieved her pain and anxiety.

The atmosphere was uplifting, as the children all freely played a part in providing the loving reassurance they felt their mother needed. This is so much easier to achieve in the environment of "home" with the familiar sounds, objects, paintings, music, and triggers for memory. The Anglican priest came and gave Peggy a prayerful blessing. All this allowed Peggy to peacefully slip away in just less than a week.

In Peggy's case I believe death was not an enemy but a welcome friend. I understand that it is difficult for a nursing home to replicate this private care. However, the principles of palliative care together with persistent reporting to doctors in charge need to be a priority of all those working in aged care settings. Referrals to palliative care teams need to come sooner rather than later, as it is well recognized that this type of care extends to all those with a life-threatening illness and not just to patients suffering from cancer.

Chronic pain is complex and Peggy had a history of neuropathic pain stemming from her decaying spine. This was not helped with the use of a lifter for showering and sitting Peggy out of bed. It was evident that Peggy was more comfortable in bed and that the gentle touch of a bed sponge would have been more appropriate. I was told by a daughter that she sensed that length of life was a priority in the nursing home and that pain relief and sedation were withheld, as they might make Peggy too drowsy to eat. These are ethical issues now being widely discussed.

I am often asked about the difference between palliative care and euthanasia. When I was presenting to a nursing home audience and talking about the butterfly and how it needs to struggle from the chrysalis so that its wings are strong enough to fly, a voice in the front row said, "We have a butterfly farm and if you try to help the butterfly from the chrysalis it dies!" I like to think of the butterfly as a person's soul or essence and the chrysalis as the body, which has served its purpose and is no longer needed. The butterfly, or soul, has work to do. For me palliative care is soul work. It is more than a purely medical solution. Euthanasia, from the Greek word meaning good death, is frequently viewed as someone other than the person in question making a decision to cease life. "Physician assisted dying" is a term used when large doses of medications are administered to bring about the death at the request of the patient. A palliative care physician may order terminal sedation when death is imminent to relieve existential and physical suffering. Who is best to decide which is the greater good for a given circumstance? It is a complex conundrum. On the subject of soul, the following authors have guided me.

David Tacey (2003) is one of Australia's leading thinkers in the areas of religion and spirituality. He says that to fall into spirituality is to fall into a larger pattern of reality, over which we have no control, and before which we stand astonished, mystified, and often disoriented. He writes that the work of the soul is largely unconscious and is related to prayer, meditation, dreams, music, poetry, and art.

Bede Griffiths (1982) was a Benedictine monk who set up an Ashram in India, which combined Christian values, and Hindu thought. He writes that it is not any particular form of religion, but religion itself, which is on trial in the modern world. He believed that only an ecumenical movement among religions, with each learning to accept and appreciate the truth and holiness to be found in the other religions, could answer the needs for religion today. He writes that Eastern traditions honor cosmic unity by which people and nature are sustained by an all-pervading spirit rather than a concept of God, who is set over the world as its creator and Lord and rules its destiny from above.

Saint Teresa of Avila was a sixteenth century saint and contemplative. Her contribution to mystical understanding was her text *The Interior Castle,* which describes a soul's journey. Her seven central ideas are described in a book written by the internationally renowned spiritual teacher, Carolyn Myss (2007):

(1) *Each of us has an outer self and an inner self;*

(2) *The inner self lives in the timeless, eternal now;*

(3) *The inner self is a great mystery, or pure emptiness and unknowingness;*

(4) *The inner self is divine, or perfectly one with infinity spirit in a supreme identity;*

(5) *Hell is identification with the outer self;*

(6) *Heaven is the discovery and realization of the inner divine self;*

(7) *The divine self is one with the all, given in grace and sealed in glory.*

Healing the soul or psyche is invisible work and therefore difficult. I have come to appreciate that clinical hypnosis and meditation are powerful ways of exploring the unconscious, which Larry Dossey, MD, author of many texts on mind and body medicine, suggests is wiser than we are and is our interface with God. He says, "I used to believe that we must choose between science and reason on one hand, and spirituality on the other, in how we lead our lives. Now I consider this a false choice. We can recover the sense of sacredness, not just in science, but in perhaps every area of life."

CHAPTER TWENTY-FOUR

Different States of Consciousness

When I first met Jimmy he was in a private hospital and had just been diagnosed with cancer. He was an electrician by trade and lived alone in a small Housing Trust home. He had two children in their early twenties. His daughter lived close by and his son needed to be traced with help from the social services to be told of his father's illness. Jimmy said his first thought when he was told of his diagnosis was that he was dead. My heart went out to this simple, honest man, and I visited him several times in hospital.

One day I found Jimmy on the floor of his room, tracing imaginary electrical wires up the leg of his over-bed table. The nursing staff reported that his behavior was due to the pain-relieving medication he had been given. Another suggestion was that the cancer had spread to the brain. Medical investigations followed and in a short space of time Jimmy was transferred to the local hospice. I reported to the staff of the hospice that his favorite food was sardine sandwiches and asked if that could be organized.

When I went to see Jimmy in the hospice, he said he was being looked after but he still dreamt about having a sardine sandwich. Probably in the life of a busy hospice this preference was overlooked for what would have seemed to be more immediate problems, such as tracing the son and attending to medical issues. The next time I visited Jimmy I took the best sardine sandwiches I could make from the freshest bread. These I served on a silver platter complete with a linen napkin and a silver fork for feeding Jimmy the bite size pieces. We shared some fun.

Jimmy had a wish to spend time at his humble home as he had gone from hospital to the hospice. The hospice was responsive to this need and an ambulance took him home where my palliative care assistants looked after him for the short time we had. His children had made a large "Welcome home" sign for his arrival. This was a valuable time for reflecting on life and preparing to leave life. However, an indwelling catheter was needed, and as Jimmy was paralyzed and a big man, caring for his pressure points was an ongoing issue and he needed more than the care we could provide at home.

On visiting Jimmy after his return to the hospice, I noticed he was not on the woolen overlay that we had donated to protect his skin. When I asked the nurse about this, she replied they were using zinc cream on his sacral area and this would mark the woolen overlay. I asked Jimmy if he was happy about that treatment or if he would like the protective occlusive dressing we were using, which wasn't harmful to the woolen overlay. I believe in giving patients choice and control where possible and including them in conversations concerning their well-being.

This was not well received by the hospice staff and I was told that I needed to speak to them away from the patient. Another time I visited and found Jimmy questioning his medications and wanting to have a say in what he was taking to make him comfortable and less anxious. At the nurses' station I praised this attitude. The nurse replied, "Why, we know best what he needs." I cannot agree with this paternalistic approach, and I believe that patient-centered care is more about a therapeutic, trusting, two-way relationship. Needs vary and are personal. Some may need to sleep more and appreciate the side effect of a medication on one occasion.

Another day may be the opposite. Preparing to die is a complicated event. There is no "one size fits all" or no clinical pathway that is straight.

This can be likened to a dance. At times the patient is taking the lead and at other times the caring team need to take the lead. I well remember Jimmy saying, when asked about his beliefs, that faith to him was like a mountain and there were many paths to the top. Some relatives of patients report that they feel left out when a clinical pathway is adhered to too rigidly. Guidance is useful but relatives and the patient need their timing respected.

Jimmy spent several weeks in the hospice. Nearing the end of his life, his bed was pushed out into the hospice garden—a lovely thing to do. A nurse who was with him made an interesting observation. She said Jimmy reported smelling smoke some time before a fire engine could be heard. This reminds me of the Buddhist teaching about the gross mind and the subtle mind. As the gross mind, which uses all the senses, diminishes, the subtle mind expands. The subtle mind may be understood as mental telepathy or a dream state as in meditation or near death. In Kadampa Buddhism, it is said that "it is the very subtle mind that will eventually transform into the omniscient mind of a Buddha."

Many who work with dying patients say that hearing is the last faculty to go. Lessons on mind states in Buddhism suggest more, and I have found reading about the Buddhist way of dying helpful. People who have experienced near-death experiences report the communication they received from loved ones or "the light" was by thought. I find that mind, psyche, soul, and spirit are all words to be explored in my individual search for meaning. I am thankful for the memory of Jimmy, who first initiated my questioning about these different states of consciousness.

CHAPTER TWENTY-FIVE

A Peaceful End

My introduction to Arthur came from an interstate phone call from one of his daughters. Apart from making an arrangement to meet at the hospital to talk about possible nursing support at home, I do not remember much about the conversation. I do remember asking if Arthur believed in a life after death or had emotional or spiritual support from a particular faith. I learned that as a pillar of society and a man of leadership he had attended church with his wife, but his daughters were left wondering how deeply church ritual had touched the core of his being.

Our meeting at the hospital took place in a visitors' room until there was the request to go to Arthur's room. He knew the meeting was planned and wanted to be included. How right! The palliative care specialist was there, too, and chuckled when I introduced myself with words that went something like this: "I'm Joy and joy by nature. I only flirt with men who are over ninety or very sick." Arthur replied with a twinkle in his eye, "I qualify on both counts!" That was the beginning of the arrangements we were to put in place to make it possible for Arthur to return to the unit that had become his home after the sale of the family home. However, he and his daughters were worried about him going home. They had thought he would stay in the local community hospital until his death. He was very comfortable there, knew some of the staff, and visitors could easily come and go. However, this was not possible when the palliative care section was closed.

Arthur's three daughters were all professionals and turned their skills to making the unit as comfortable as possible. An electric hospital bed was placed in the main room so that there was room for visitors and a connection with his much loved rose garden from the windows and the sounds of traffic in the street. As soon as he was installed in this very comfortable bed, it was clear the choice was right. Favorite small meals were planned and paperwork attended to. Arthur had always been a skilled and meticulous manager of his business affairs and was comforted by seeing that things were being handled according to his usual practice and standards. Grandchildren and great grandchildren came to visit. Several doctors were in the family as well as Arthur's grounded, supportive sister. Neighbors learned that Arthur was home and came to pay their respects and chat. He could eat and drink whatever he liked whenever he chose. He could sleep when tired, undisturbed by hospital routines. It was his own home and he was able to have a level of control. The family felt it was a very good move.

Arthur knew that his life was hanging by a thread, and as nurses and palliative care assistants, we tried to attend to "normal" nursing duties such as hygiene and skin and bowel care. We soon realized that activities as showering and getting out of bed to a commode for bowel care were putting too much stress on Arthur's heart. In order not to break the incredible atmosphere in the room with a sudden death, these activities gave way to a bed sponge, a urinary drainage catheter, gentle turns for skin care, mouth care, and forgetting about evacuating the bowel. Arthur's demands for his favorite foods continued and there was shared delight in delivering his requests.

Arthur was over ninety and had multiple physical ailments and an ambiguous diagnosis of bowel complications, kidney failure, and heart failure. He was proud of his naval career, his business career, his successful share trading, and his contribution to various boards and to the aged care complex where his wife had lived with him until her death. At the funeral, I learned about the activities he had initiated for the family when they were young. He was clever and fully engaged in life, yet death was a big step for him and those present. He had little acute pain but became more uncomfortable with being bedbound and having our palliative care assistants roll him from side to side. Medication was introduced for physical and emotional comfort.

One day I visited and shared the story of Peter, who had died the previous night. In the chapter in this book dedicated to Peter, I tell of using hypnosis to take him up in a special white plane and, having tested his parachute, to jump so that he could see his old self (body no longer needed) parachuting to earth and his true self piloting the plane onwards. Arthur said, "I like that!" I said that maybe his image could be pulling up anchor. I know that Arthur had a church funeral and was anointed and had regular Holy Communion in his last weeks.

Loving care continued, and it seemed that Arthur had pushed the "pause" button on the story of his life as he indulged in the attention being given to him. He wound down slowly as all stress was removed from his body and psyche. Love conquers all. Oral medication became a burden and new medications were given by a subcutaneous infusion. The doctors in the family made sure that he had the best medication to keep him comfortable, to avoid the noisy breathing that is often described as "death rattles," and to be present until all the family felt that it was time to put his needs above their own and let him slip away.

During the vigil that followed the increase in medication, there was a powerful sense of love and feeling of the presence of spirit. Breakthrough medication was given more frequently to make sure that

Arthur's physical body was as comfortable as possible. Arthur's sister and family were all united in wishing him a good voyage.

I was not present when Arthur's breathing gently stopped but I understand it was a profoundly peaceful moment. The daughters stayed the night in the unit with Arthur's body, as did our palliative care assistant. I arrived in the morning just after the funeral people had taken Arthur's body away. I collected our nursing equipment, connected with the daughters and left feeling proud that this dignified vessel of a man had sailed confidently away to other shores.

CHAPTER TWENTY-SIX

Seeing Soul

Sophia was in hospital when I first met her. She had a nasty ovarian cancer that had spread widely and she was questioning the usefulness of her medical treatments, which had so many discomforts attached to them. She wanted to talk about dying. She wanted to hear of my experiences and to talk about beliefs around dying and what happens after death. I was summoned weekly for about six weeks. She had only one son who was the apple of her eye. Like her, he was a lawyer. Her husband, who was the love of her life, had died several years before. She was seventy and until recently had been working assisting people who could not afford to pay for their legal representation.

In one of our chats about death and dying, she asked me to assist her in writing a letter to her oncologist and her son. She wanted to express, without emotion, her feelings that she was preparing to die and felt the treatment she was receiving was distracting from the process of letting go of this known world. The treatments made her so nauseous and the benefits were difficult to discern. She was continuing to experience pain and was slowly realizing that the prospects of living with any quality of life were fading. In this letter she wanted to not only express how she felt, but also to protect and honor the integrity of her doctor, who was trying everything to halt the spread of her cancer, and to build on her relationship with her son. She didn't want her giving up treatment to be seen by either as a lack of appreciation for their care and encouragement or her not trying hard enough to get better. As an individual, she wanted this time to be hers.

While we talked I massaged her hands and feet and I felt connected to this intelligent woman in an irrational and deep way. She shared that when she was young and living in Europe she had been interested in spiritualism and the rituals that embedded in her intuitive insights into another world or mode of existence. This seemed a strange interest for someone who had a legal mind and occupation. It reminded me of the time I lived in England before I was married and became familiar with the work of Betty Shine, a prolific writer, who was a mind and energy healer advocating the power of visualization and positive psychology. We shared an interest in Betty Shine's work and in how healing is not only to be found within a medical model that concentrates on the physical body.

Yet it was a struggle for Sophia to discontinue the treatments being offered to her and to prepare to die. She did not find comfort in a traditional religion, but she did practice meditation and played a CD of Buddhist chanting to assist her in being transported beyond her painful physical body. As a Reiki practitioner, I felt guided in our interactions. She was interested in a course I had recently completed on chakra cleansing, which clears the blocks that energy may encounter as it courses through the body. During one of our sessions, I told her of an image given to me by a friend who is a Catholic nun. This image is of a parachute and the message below it is: the mind is like a parachute—it functions best when fully open.

When the hospital was no longer an option because of private health insurance constraints, Sophia was forced to continue her journey at home. During her time in hospital she had many visitors and these strong friendships were life-sustaining. As her treatments were reduced, pain relief was increased and medication was added for side effects and anxiety. Sophia's son and his wife came to live with her for whatever time she had left. Specially trained palliative care assistants stayed with Sophia overnight, administering medications, mopping her brow, moistening her mouth, and generally attending to the needs of her body and soul.

The bedroom had a surreal atmosphere. There was soothing music but also vibration from CDs of chanting and drumming. All this was changing and deepening Sophia's level of consciousness. There were times when she asked for toast and vegemite and a cup of tea, but mostly she chose to concentrate on the task at hand which was to die with grace and dignity. My role was to practice what I had learned, but largely not understood, from my course in chakra cleansing. I performed this ritual with the intention of honoring the unseen world and to be a calm, loving presence. People came and people went. Sophia's son and his wife served food and drinks to visitors. Everyone wanted explanations and progress reports. Progress reports are usually about getting better while our explanations could only reflect intentions.

When death did occur, I remember standing in the dimly lit room, feeling very still in my body and gazing at the wall above Sophia's head. I saw an orb of light about ten centimeters in diameter rise from her head and travel towards the ceiling. I noticed that the main orb of light was partly hiding another orb of light. This image slowly rose to the ceiling and disappeared. I felt in awe and wished that I had taken a photograph. I looked for a source that could have reflected this light but there was none. It was daylight; the room was shielded from outside light and there were flickering candles, which could not have reflected the symmetrical balls of light I saw. Sophia had talked much about her husband and the closeness they shared. I wondered if he had come to get her.

CHAPTER TWENTY-SEVEN

A Gift to a Granddaughter

Malcolm was a heart specialist who retired early and became a great cook. His wife was not fond of cooking and Malcolm found that cooking the evening meal was a practical gift to his bridge-playing wife. He was meticulous with following a recipe and had an eye for presentation. When I met him he had days to live, and like with everything else in his life this time needed order. He subjected himself to the cancer treatments mainly, I was told, to protect and look after his wife. This changed when one day he begged his daughter to take him out of hospital and to his beautiful Victorian style home in a delightful garden setting.

That was when I met the family who had called me in for a family meeting. They were keen to follow their father's wishes, but this was uncharted waters for them and Malcolm had been in charge of his medications and in charge generally. I was told he was sleeping a lot and had trouble passing his urine. We had discussions, which gave the family members the opportunity to voice how they saw the current situation and what their feelings were about it being time to be without their beloved Malcolm. There was general agreement that the kindest thing to do would be to have an honest conversation with Malcolm in which they all said that while he would be missed, they would feel better if he was not suffering anymore.

I was taken in to meet Malcolm in his downstairs bedroom. The family had spared no effort to accommodate his failing health. There was equipment in adequate supply. Malcolm smiled as I introduced myself and told him he was known for his work as a physician. He seemed happy to see me and I like to think he knew I would also care for his family. I could see he was used to self-medicating, as there were pills on the bedside table. I could also see his main discomfort was a full bladder. Where to turn for help? Being a physician, a general practitioner or family doctor didn't play a large part in Malcolm's health management. There were always specialist friends to ask for advice.

The family had requested a meeting after 5:00 PM to suit their work responsibilities; it was now 7:00 PM and I needed help to insert a male catheter and to assess what medications were needed. I phoned a general practitioner who had said he would help with my patients if it was appropriate and in his area. I went back to the office where nursing supplies for catheterization were kept and the delightful general practitioner came and together we changed Malcolm's life to a degree. A large amount of urine was drained and the relief from the discomfort of a full to overflowing bladder had to be enormous. The kindly general practitioner was certainly appreciated and together we tried to work out what medications would maintain a state of comfort for the rest of the night. A palliative care assistant was called to give the family a worry-reduced night. To have help when needed is truly patient-centered care. Seldom do the needs of the patient or family fit into office hours or are able to be anticipated.

During the night it was reported that Malcolm had required considerable medication by way of sleeping tablets and tablets for pain. When shown the shoebox of medications prescribed for Malcolm, the family and doctor realized he had been covering up quite a bit of discomfort. A brave face and positive attitude can hide much. It was clear that further radiation treatment would be more of a burden than a benefit and that Malcolm had been right in making the decision to "just go home." It must have been an enormous relief for him to have his family, a delightful doctor, and practical nursing support enveloping him with all this love and attention and in his own "castle."

It is always difficult in this kind of emergency to know what medications to put into a syringe driver and what doses. Sensibly, the doctor ordered baseline medications for pain relief and calming medication and wrote orders for breakthrough medication to be given as needed. The family needed to mentally adjust to the fact that Malcolm would soon die. Yes, they were pleased to have him home and knew they were supporting his wishes. But this time of preparation is about much more than thinking rationally; it is also a time of euphoria when nothing seems real. The family members went through the motions of daily living while phoning his many friends. The power of thought is very strong and I feel that the energy from well-wishers can be felt by the person whose energy is preparing to leave the body.

Malcolm was being nursed in a double bed. This meant that his wife and family could lie beside him in the old familiar ways. Too often, in my opinion, a practical hospital bed is advised. Yes, they have a place when the patient is immobile, heavy, and perhaps in a coma, but a familiar bed of one's own is a comfort not to be forgotten. I remember one hospital patient discharged to home where a hospital bed was recommended and it was not appreciated. That man had just met the love of his life who had been a childhood sweetheart and whom fate had separated him from for some seventy years. Soon after their marriage the man suffered from a terminal illness and the time available for them to be together was days. I remember his smile well when, with the help of several burley friends, he was carried on a sheet to the large bed where he and his soul mate could spend much time lying side by side.

Joy Nugent

For Malcolm, medications were titrated to fit his personal needs. There were times when he wanted to be more awake to enjoy his grandchildren and visitors, and there were times when he sought peace and quiet. The time of death is difficult to predict, as it would seem that so much of what is happening is unconscious. For Malcolm's last night his son's daughter had offered to stay with Malcolm's wife for support. The palliative care assistant was in harmony with her patient's needs and tidied the room as if to create sacred space for this man to die. My role was to be available by telephone if there was a concern. When Malcolm's breathing changed she went to advise the granddaughter, who came to the bedside in time to see her grandfather sit up and look at her with wide open eyes before taking his final breath, resting back on the pillows. She said it was a moment of awe and I said that it was a gift.

When I went to see the family the next morning, Malcolm had been dead for perhaps eight hours. I was amazed to see a smile fixed on his face. He looked happy! As is so often the case, those caring for the person at this time learn so much at the funeral. Malcolm's funeral was well attended, and the stories told by his male friends caused many a chuckle. There were slides of the extravagant family Christmas celebrations with various dress-up themes. He was a character larger than life but also one who had experienced leaving the country of his birth, settling in a strange environment and succeeding on his own from his teenage years. He had reached the pinnacle of his medical profession and had made his home his last port of call.

CHAPTER TWENTY-EIGHT

Dying in Character

Iain was country gentry and lived in the home his parents had lived in with his wife, Bryony. Their interests were in sheep when there was a market for wool and now cattle and horses. The house was no longer an example of splendor with its tennis court, covered swimming pool, and pine tree lined driveway in need of repair and maintenance. Iain was not one to spend money on "show." One of his daughters prepared a room for him at the end of the large house when the decision was made for Iain to come home from an acute care hospital after he was diagnosed with an inoperable blood clot in his neck following a stroke. His hired hospital bed was placed in front of a large famous Australian landscape painting with a simple wooden frame. The room was sunlit and cozy with a wood-fired heater and roses from an unkempt garden just showing above the windowsill.

Iain was in his mid-seventies and proud of his four children. Bryony remarked that it took four children to look after the property. The children were all married and with families of their own. They all came forward to support their father. After the stroke, swallowing became difficult and Iain bravely resisted the offer of a feeding tube via his nose for some time. He could still talk and make his wishes known. The daughter who contacted me said her father was a very pragmatic man and one to have definite views on what was an acceptable way of life when he could no longer be independent. He had been diagnosed with an incurable neurological disease some years prior to the stroke and had a heart problem. These conditions gave him time to formulate his values. He was close to nature with his animals, trees, and garden. He loved horses and was pleased to boast of a daughter's interest in riding. He also loved champagne and Guinness!

Bryony was a charming and supportive mate who I suspect followed her husband's lead in all things related to the family. She did not enjoy good health and appreciated the family taking charge at this important time. There were many conversations with one particular daughter about the possibility of her father dying at home. There was also a phone conversation with Iain's son, who questioned why his father refused the feeding tube and any further treatment. Could it be seen as giving up in this final battle to stay alive? My sense was that it could be giving false hope, as there was no chance of Iain recovering to the point of independent living. I saw the decision as a brave one, but as so often happens a parent will try to please a child. A tube was inserted twice, and twice Iain pulled it out. Apparently a circumstance such as this had been discussed earlier with all concerned, and Iain had made his wish clear that he did not wish to end up in a nursing home dependent on others for his bodily care.

The day I visited him in hospital was the day he was offered a small amount of puréed food by mouth. He took a little, I believe, but he was still keen to go home and not pursue any more treatment. At home he would be offered whatever he fancied. One day it was his favorite dessert, which was lovingly prepared but not eaten; another day it was his favorite fish dish, which he requested but only managed a small taste. Guinness was offered by way of a small syringe, and finally jumbo swabs were dipped in Guinness and frozen as an alternative to ice chips.

Once Iain was settled at home, visitors started to arrive and were made welcome. At first the caring team maintained support on a twenty-four hour basis, but this was soon reduced to overnight and morning with the family and friends taking care of the afternoon. This was made possible with medication given via a subcutaneous infusion. Pain was the main discomfort, and although Iain was on an alternating pressure mattress, repositioning was painful. I learned that there was a history of pain coming from pinched nerves in his neck. His good shoulder also became painful, and we wondered if it could have been injured during his fall when the stroke occurred some two weeks prior. It had not been x-rayed. A urinary drainage catheter was offered and rejected, as was any effort to open his bowels. One of our palliative care assistants was a strong but gentle energy therapist and could have assisted in lifting Iain onto a commode, but Iain showed no interest. He just wanted to lie still and have as much comfortable time as possible with his family and friends.

This continued for a week, although there were long spells when Iain was asleep. The first night home was difficult for him and he experienced the all-too-familiar restlessness and trouble with clearing his throat. Intermittent medications were given but it became clear that a small dose of continuous medication would maintain comfort. Prior to turning or washing, pain-relieving medication and medication for calming were given.

There were several times when those present believed that Iain was dying. Family were called from far and wide. Judging the time to call relatives is always difficult. I see the psyche needing time to heal just as the body does. The dream state seems to be more active and surprising events occur. At one stage, Iain suddenly sat bolt upright from a coma-like state before settling into a restful sleep. From a nursing point of view, I was pleased that the bed rails were up although it was hardly likely that this semi-paralysed man could be in danger of having a fall.

During this vigil period Iain's son arrived and gave his mother special attention. Together they went for a long walk around the property. The weather was perfect and although the air was fresh, it was decided that the wood-fired heater needed to stay on to make sure the man at the center of all this attention was kept warm. At one stage he became too warm with wheat bags on his shoulder as well as the fire. The intention was certainly to be attentive to all areas of his comfort. When I first met Iain he told me that the champagne that bore my name was too expensive, but he suggested that when it was time I was to give a bottle to his wife. The day before he died I arrived with a bottle of "Joy" sparkling wine in my hand. It was as though I was keeping my side of the bargain.

The evening Iain died all the children were present, and I am told they toasted his passing with "Joy." The palliative care assistant who was present said that when it came time to give Iain his final wash and to dress him everyone wanted to help. During his week at home he had insisted on being dressed in his shirt rather than pajamas. To do this, the sleeves and the back of the shirt were cut. No matter, he looked good from the front! His wife also cut his hair and he was frequently shaved with his electric shaver. After death he was dressed in all his favourite brand clothing, and when I went to visit the next morning I saw a man with a proud pose who was dressed in style. What a wonderful death the family had given him! I was told that it was what they had wanted to do but needed a bit of support and mentoring. The general practitioner was also very supportive and came to do home visits. It makes me wonder why so many people outsource this last phase of life to health professionals and institutions and why conversations around advance care directives are so difficult. This personalized death could not have happened in the hospital ward where the staff was cautious about his discharge.

CHAPTER TWENTY-NINE

Fear-based Care

I was asked by the daughters of a ninety-four-year-old woman to make a nursing home visit to see their mother, Joan. It was their intention to support her in every way so that she could experience a dignified death. For some months Joan had been saying that she wanted to die. She was very frail, she was bed-bound, and her body was wasting away. She had pain from arthritis and suffered all the other discomforts of an aging body. She was being nursed on an alternating pressure mattress in a hospital bed. The nursing staff said the woman had been very depressed, but the daughters did not feel that their mother was depressed at all. It seemed to me, from listening to the nursing staff, that for someone to welcome death they had to have a mental health problem. Surely if the fear of death could be removed, every resident would welcome death when they felt it was their time. Death doesn't need to be seen as the enemy or as a failure of medical science.

To my questioning, the nurse in charge repeated, "We do not do euthanasia here." For many the word "euthanasia" means "mercy killing." In my view this was not a case of mercy killing but rather a rational request for a supported, pain-free transition from this world to the next. Nurses and doctors assist with the birth of a baby at the beginning of life. Is that so different to assisting in a process where energy leaves a body at the end of life? Death for Joan was not an enemy but a welcome friend. The nurse in charge said she was uncomfortable with a palliative care approach, as the patient didn't have a disease that was life threatening. An outside palliative team visited and the doctor ordered pain relief to be given hourly if necessary. He also ordered medication for anxiety to be given hourly if needed and some oral drops to be administered for sedation. It seemed with these orders that every discomfort had been considered to give this elderly patient a good death. Family were supportive, understanding, and in attendance, and they were striving to advocate for their mother.

So what caused so much distress among the nursing staff? Attitude, knowledge, and skills need constant evaluation. Death is more than a medical and nursing issue. It is about the soul and the meaning of life. This will vary for everyone, but just as different religions need respect, so do the different beliefs and values of individuals. Withdrawing from food and fluid is part of the dying process, yet this frail lady was repositioned for feeding at meal times as if death was not an option. When asked about food, one of my elderly patients said, "My body doesn't need food anymore."

The body is much less important during the terminal phase of life. It needs to be kept pain-free and comfortable so the soul can prepare to leave. That was the metaphor I used in a brief session of hypnosis with Joan. She apparently loved roses, and I suggested we visit her garden in her mind's eye and walk around it, observing and appreciating the flowers. The script included seeing a caterpillar climbing up a long rose stem and turning into a chrysalis, and when nature timed the event a butterfly would emerge from its discarded shell like a soul leaving the body to fly free and to soar to the light. On returning to this world Joan said, "That was beautiful!" We spoke about her life and she told me she wanted to join her husband and her parents. They were good people, and she still felt a connection with them. This is not mercy killing!

Joan had a feeling deep in her soul that it was her time, and she was in a loving state. Why was this a cause to be frightened of the effects of medications? The intention of the family was clearly to support their mother. The nurses were terrified of being found negligent in their duty of care by giving pain relief when the patient was sleeping and not complaining. The principle of pain relief is surely to get ahead of pain and discomfort by giving a continuous infusion of medication and not wait until the patient is screaming. The problem was that the breakthrough orders were for "as needed" and relied on a judgment of observable physical distress.

This was not the case with all of the nurses so sometimes the medication for comfort was given and sometimes it was not, depending on the confidence of the nurse and requests from the family. The daughters told me that the visitor from the palliative care service was a social worker and they questioned her competency in the area of medication. Trust, which is an important factor in care, was broken between the family and those caring. This was so much so that the family wanted their mother moved to a hospice. There appears to be confusion about what is "hospice care" and what is "palliative care." While both are intended to relieve suffering, hospice care provides care for people in the last phases of an incurable disease so that they may live as fully and comfortably as possible. Palliative care focuses on helping patients get relief from symptoms caused by serious illness and is appropriate at any age or stage in a serious illness.

What is the future for residents in aged care facilities? Certainly, the conversations around advance care directives are making a small difference in empowering patients to cease taking what is intended to be life-prolonging medication. Strangely, when the decision to cease medications is taken, reports from nursing staff and families often confirm that the patient feels better! Medication is only part of the answer to maintaining a healthy body. For holistic practitioners, mind, body, and spirit all interact. Yes, pay attention to the body, but also make time to feel connected to the cycles of nature, to practice calming the mind, and to reflect on life in a positive way. There are many lessons to be learned by being in tune with people at the end of their life. Conquering personal fears is a first step.

It was interesting to hear Joan's two daughters reassure their mother that her genes would live on through them and their children. This is comfort for many, but I reminded them that their mother believed she would be with her husband and parents. "Being with" can take many forms and adds to the questions that arise during bedside discussions. Many people just want to leave everything to the doctor and to those who purport to know best. The trouble is that trusted doctors get sick and take holidays and chosen family advocates are not always available. I still hear that sometimes wishes are recorded in Wills, which are not read until after death. There still seems to be a widely held belief that it is not the time to think about dying matters.

CHAPTER THIRTY

Reconnecting with the Church

Jonathan was in his mid-fifties when he died. He had been a successful businessman with connections in many countries. He had mesothelioma and wasn't giving in to the disease without a fight. When I met him he lived in a large modern house with a sculptured garden along with his eldest daughter, who was studying for a degree in accounting. His three other children lived with their mother. The parents were divorced and the process had been bitter. Jonathan's work took him away from home for long periods and may have contributed to the breakdown of the marriage. Like so many men with high mental capacity, Jonathan's communication of emotions and feelings was not a strong attribute. The emotional scars were evident in his children's behavior. Children are often the ones to suffer when strong emotions are felt but not understood.

Wealthy, handsome men attract women, and several attempted to win Jonathan's heart after the divorce. One did succeed and became his muse. After several years of inspirational living, Jonathan's muse developed a brain tumor. His blissful world was shattered. There followed every medical intervention from far and wide only to end in her death. She was buried in a country grave and Jonathan would confide that her spirit was felt in those quiet moments before sleep. I never asked if he hoped to see her again in spirit form. In spite of the futile efforts he made to keep his muse alive, Jonathan went down the same path with his diagnosis of mesothelioma. However, there seemed to be a need to be doing something rather than waiting calmly for a disease to disable his body entirely. I remember him saying he was trying his best for his mother, who spoke to him often from another state. I would give him a mother's hug on saying good-bye and could feel his deep need for such non-judgmental loving.

In the early months of Jonathan's illness and while he was seeking treatment from medical trials, a palliative care assistant would go to the house around 6:00 PM to cook a family meal. It was important for this ritual to continue, although his daughter frequently ate out and the children who lived with their mother came and went. There were times when the palliative care assistants prepared special health foods for Jonathan. He was very particular about the purity of what he ate and that was part of his efforts not to let his mother down. The disease and nausea took their toll in the end and fortified liquids became the norm. In spite of extreme weakness, Jonathan insisted on attending to his daily hygiene and being as independent as possible. Perhaps it was only weeks before his death that he asked the priest from a nearby parish to visit. It was his wish to be reconciled with his Christian faith, which was also the faith of his mother. His parents, although divorced, came together at the funeral to offer the bread and wine for the sacrament of communion. If Jonathan's spirit was present, he would have been pleased to see his mother receive the support she did.

Jonathan would have also been pleased to see his mates, who had supported him through thick and thin, continue to support his children and even their mother. The eulogy had an international flavor and it was clear that this businessman was admired by many and for much. They were all connected through business, and while one helped him to the toilet in a very weak state, others were there visiting and caring for the family. What a tangled web is woven with the breakup of a family unit. Now the mother of the children visited and the younger children were encouraged to join in with the care of their father. Even after death they touched him and laid with him. Words of healing and forgiveness are often heard in the lead up to death. The visit by the priest and the planning of the requiem mass were acts of this man, who had fought a good fight and showed courage by example.

I remember assisting with washing Jonathan's hair in bed and he expressed his extreme fear while his body lay curled in the fetal position. He had requested one last night in his own bed before being transferred to a hospital bed with its alternating pressure mattress. Now it was time to transfer to that bed and it became a huge hurdle in the mind of this man facing death. In striving to give comfort and knowing that Jonathan had spent time in the east, I said that if he had ever considered reincarnation I was sure he would come back a warlord. That made him smile. We did need to give him some anti-anxiety medication before our male palliative care assistant and a son could transfer Jonathan, via a wheelchair, to the waiting hospital bed. It was as if this act was another step closer to a final good-bye.

If one looks closely at the nursing care given in the terminal phase of life, rituals can be observed that in their own way give support—not just physically but also spiritually. The giving of food is an act that changes from the intention to nourish the body to keeping the mouth moist and refreshing memories. Hygiene changes from standing in the shower independently to being hand washed and bathed in bed. Shaving changes to the use of an electric razor so that others can do the task. Catheters and incontinence products replace the act of "going to the toilet." Bowel care is forgotten in the last days of life. Perfumes and essential oils are sourced to add to the aromas of skin lotions, as if the body is being anointed in some way. The entertainment provided by the media, while providing a sense of normality, also needs to change to what soothes and relaxes—the football gives way to the Gregorian chant or Beethoven's requiem. Maybe these actions in some way anoint the soul of the person, as do the sacraments provided by the church.

As society becomes more secular and many people are finding the kingdom of God within as well as without, it is important to add new rituals to replace discarded religious rituals. This is an important role for palliative care to embrace.

CHAPTER THIRTY-ONE

Sherry in the Cupboard

When I first met Veronica I found her in a disheveled state and still in her nightdress at 11:00 AM. There was a suspicious wet patch on the floor on the way to the bathroom and she couldn't remember who I was or why I was in her nursing home room. I told her she had phoned me on the recommendation of her sister-in-law and that perhaps I could support her in some way or take her for outings? She considered this but it was not until I picked up some pages covered in handwriting that she became interested. "That is my book," she said. "I am rewriting it as I threw the first attempt away." I offered to help her and said that I could bring my laptop computer with me next time I came to visit. Having awakened her interest in living, she also said she would love to go to her old hairdresser in a nearby suburb.

It was arranged that one of our palliative care assistants (PCA) would accompany Veronica in a special cab to her hair appointment. There was an initial fuss at the nursing home, where the employees wanted her to go in a wheelchair and to be assessed by the physiotherapist. This was a sensible suggestion but not one that was acceptable to Veronica. Pride and a strong will can do wonders! The words, "Where there is a will, there is a way," have much merit. From her first visit to the hairdresser and to what was a feature of her life prior to being in the nursing home, she became a changed woman. She was a born flirt and her hairdresser was charming. Such a little thing as a hair appointment resulted in so much pleasure. From that day we would visit and take her out two or three times a week. She found jewelry that she wanted fixed, clothes that needed to be altered, and food treats to share with her palliative care assistant. She visited the Indian shop in the shopping center and bought cheap rings to add to her sapphire engagement ring. All of this was done with the assistance of a walking frame and determination! The walking frame had a seat that lifted up to reveal a pocket for her money and purchases. She frequently bought packets of sweets for the other residents. In many ways she was the "duchess archetype" and saw herself as a cut above the other residents. She found meaning in looking after these elderly people. She did not see herself as one of them.

On the days that I visited, Veronica would produce pages of handwritten notes for me to record with the assistance of my computer. We would work for just over an hour, sharing the stories of her early life. Then she would produce two sherry glasses, a bottle of sherry, an avocado, two teaspoons, and a bottle of salad dressing. This was our feast. It reminded me of boarding school and breaking rules. This continued for several years and it was hard to recall the same woman who greeted me on our first meeting. This strong individual, who suffered mood swings and visited a psychologist for calming techniques, was not a typical nursing home patient. It is a common story, as she was admitted with her ninety-year-old husband after she had a fall in the bathroom of their town house and their children feared that the time had come when they could not live alone safely.

The nursing home accommodated Veronica's needs as best they could. She had been a great gardener and one morning she rose very early and planted a newly prepared small circular garden bed with her favorite Plumbago shrub. She told me that she was restricted with what she could do in the nursing home setting but thought if the bed was planted it would be left to thrive. It did. She had bought the plants on one of her outings and kept them in her bathroom. Such was the spirit of this woman! Veronica spoke a lot about her parents and was particularly fond of her mother, who taught her to play the piano. Her early childhood, boarding school, ballet, first love, and first job were all chapters in her book. She was on her way to London and drama school when the war broke out and her father ordered her to return. What a privilege it was for me to hear about this life of excitement—and there was the sherry in the cupboard for a celebratory nip.

All these reminiscent talks made Veronica yearn to revisit the Blue Mountains where she holidayed as a young person with her parents. Veronica's family was very supportive of what seemed to be an outlandish idea that a nursing home patient be allowed to go on a holiday. After all, she was incontinent and was on medication for her heart and other ailments. The nurse in charge expressed her concern about the journey from Adelaide to Sydney and beyond. I reassured her that I was a palliative care nurse and even if she died I would cope. She didn't die, and I have the most beautiful photo of her licking an ice cream cone while waiting to go on an evening cruise around Sydney Harbour—a far cry from being confined to a nursing home routine! I could do this because I practice as a private palliative care nurse and do not depend on employment by a health organization. My independent spirit appreciated the spirit of this woman in her eighties who wrote astute letters to the editors of newspapers and magazines. Her education was another story, as she had returned to university in her sixties to study English and was stimulated by the minds of fellow students and teachers.

Veronica dressed immaculately and offended the air steward by applying nail varnish on the plane. She was proud of her painted nails.

Her room was full of photos of her family. She loved classical music, and while dementia was evident she could still push the correct button to play her favorite CDs. When her husband died in the same nursing home, she moved into his room, as it was one that enjoyed sunshine. She had the birdbath from her old garden placed outside her window so she could see it and the statue of Wendy that was elegantly perched on the rim. Her favorite books were in the room in a small bookcase. Above her bed was a photo of her mother.

Veronica's husband had died soon after I met her and she wrote about the experience in a sensitive and beautiful way. We often talked about dying, and she left orders for the music she wanted played at her funeral and where she wanted to be buried. Yet it would be another year before she had attended to all her "unfinished business," which mainly involved her four children. As one child said, "It was always difficult to know whether it was our real mother talking to us or an actress playing the part of a mother." Romantic she was, but also talented and intelligent.

Veronica's dementia increased and my visits ceased once her memoirs reached marriage and a move to a new city. It seemed that the time of life when she felt most herself had needed to be revisited and written about. There were exciting times of love and laughter during these sessions. She said she always dreamed of being rich and famous. As part of our outings we visited the homes she had lived in. Not content with the view from the road, she would want to meet the current owners.

On one shopping trip to buy a new blouse Veronica had the shop attendant bring the item of clothing to the footpath where it was easier for her to balance on her walking frame. There were other trips to a florist to send flowers to a grandchild. These outings were all shadows of her former lifestyle. One Anzac Day she ordered a taxi to take her to the parade. Her orders included passing a barrier to the general public by announcing, "I am the wife of ... and insist on being close to the laying of wreaths." She got her wish and somehow made her way back to the nursing home! Obviously her children had given permission for outings, but I wondered if this permission included going out by herself. Veronica's husband had been a decorated soldier whom she met in the islands off New Guinea while working for the Red Cross. That was another chapter we wrote amid chuckles caused by her adventures with the soldiers.

All this reminiscence makes me wonder how well nursing home patients in general are prepared for their last phase of life. So often I hear encouragement to join a bus outing, play bingo, or join other group activities, but what about the individual exploring their soul's journey? Talking about funeral planning, biographies, eulogies, and how a person seeks to be remembered are necessary conversations in preparing for "the end." Certainly there is the need for standards, patient's rights, accreditation, and a range of assessments, but what of love, laughter, and the sherry in the cupboard?

CHAPTER THIRTY-TWO

Hospice in Place

When I was asked to see David he was in a double nursing home room with his wife, Anne. He was elderly and suffered with chronic heart failure and Non-Hodgkin's lymphoma, but it was his activities in retirement from his work as a highly respected physician that astounded me. Anne had suffered a massive stroke some years before and David was there, not only for his own needs, but also to be near her. They had two daughters and a son who was a country general practitioner. These children had been raised by a mother who was profoundly deaf and a father with a "can do" attitude to life who had confidently climbed cliffs and pruned the tall trees in his garden without fear.

Reflecting on the lives of these two people, I am in awe of their characters. They were both university students when Anne became totally deaf from treatment received for an illness. They enjoyed their shared interests and were in love. Anne offered to break off their relationship so as not to be a handicap to David and his work, but David would have none of it. And so they began their life together in a lasting and rewarding marriage. The children learned to get their mother's attention by tugging at her skirt, and she was adamant that she wouldn't use sign language, as she wanted to be part of the hearing community. I understand that she depended solely on lip-reading and was an expert. The children said, "To communicate, we had to face her and speak very clearly so she could understand us."

A comfortable and productive way of life continued, and when Anne was in her fifties she became the first South Australian to have a cochlear implant. Before Anne became deaf she used to attend concerts. However, I was told by the family that she wrote in Professor Graeme Clark's (inventor of the bionic ear) book "this new language ... can be crackly, squeaky, resonant, piercing ... and music holds no pleasure," but she did agree that, "Friends seem to have become more relaxed and chatty, so conversations are more normal." The implant made communication easier. It enabled Anne to have a much easier time when chatting to people and she even managed to talk on the phone for the first time in thirty-five years. However, her subsequent stroke made any form of communication difficult.

Anne's stroke had left her paralyzed down one side, unable to talk or care for herself. Although most people who suffer such a stroke would be cared for in a nursing home from the start, this was not an option for David. He was frail himself, but he had great spirit and would not be easily defeated by a challenge. For eight years he looked after his "gorgeous Annie" at home. This meant attending to all her needs, from dressing to toileting, which must have been difficult for him as his own health was poor. What an act of love!

The children told me that during this time David and Anne went for drives in their car most days and watched the sunset most evenings. David also loved to "zoom" Anne around in their double gopher, which he named "The Zinger." The picture the children painted was of him steering with one hand while having his other arm around Anne. Anne would be clinging with her one functioning hand onto the handle for dear life. They had multiple adventures—getting stuck in the middle of major roads in peak hour traffic, knocking down a food stand or two in the local supermarket, as well as many rides up to a local rose garden. What togetherness! No wonder they were well-known in the district.

This committed life was shared and enjoyed until David's deteriorating health signaled that the time had come for his beloved wife to be cared for in a nursing home. David would only let her go if he went, too. When Anne moved to high care accommodation in a nursing home, David moved into an independent unit close by. I was told that this arrangement lasted until David became gravely ill. That is where I found him, sharing a nursing home room with his wife. There he rested comfortably, listening to his music, gazing at bunches of flowers brought from his garden and chatting quietly with his family and dearest friends.

Sometimes I would visit two or three times a week. Family photographs were often prompts and the topics we covered included profound aspects of life and living. Some of my initial visits included David's children. A general practitioner was attached to the nursing home so it was easy to build a doctor, patient, and nurse relationship. David said he didn't need a palliative care specialist, as he was happy with his general practitioner. It was, however, daunting for me to have such a knowledgeable and esteemed patient to support in his end of life process. The role I tried to play was to be a sounding board for the feelings of all concerned and to facilitate comfort in a process that involves body, mind, and soul. David's body was made comfortable with a continuous infusion of medications ordered by the general practitioner, his mind's questions were answered as far as my own questioning of life's meaning would permit, his soul was affirmed with many loving actions, and those present were encouraged to be calm and keep their thoughts positive. Love and laughter mostly filled the room.

Yet it was not an easy time. David was worried about his lack of bowel movements. This is a common concern, and for me it relates to the notion of seeking to be totally prepared for the final journey. I am reminded of a saying that was often quoted to me as a child: cleanliness is next to godliness. To complement the care being given by the nursing home, I arranged for a Nepalese nurse to spend the nights with David. What a night the first night was! David's body was made clean inside and out, as well as having a genuinely caring, skillful nurse for company. It is so important to have a calm and reassuring presence with those who are dying. This is especially so at night, as people frequently die in the early hours of the morning. It is also when the dream state is most active, which can be scary unless one has a deep understanding of the unconscious and the purpose of dreams.

There was a profound moment the night before David died. David and Anne were both supporters of their church and the family organized for their minister to come to say prayers for David. The minister was in a Nepalese restaurant at the time of the phone call. The Nepalese influence was being felt in many directions. The moments of prayer were spine-tingling and seemed so timely. Where possible, Anne was included in this support for David, and her wheelchair was brought close to the bed for handholding as a means of direct communication. I'm sure they were joined at a soul level.

A few months after David died, Anne's health also deteriorated. The children recall that when she developed pneumonia, they spent the night with her in the emergency department of a city hospital. Despite being so ill, this spirited soul still managed a little smile whenever she opened her eyes and saw her children sitting next to her. They told me that at one point she looked over to the wall of her cubicle. Something had very obviously caught her attention. It was just a dingy blank wall—nothing there—but she stared intently at it and looked over to those present with her dark eyes wide open in amazement. It seemed that her questioning eyes were asking if anyone else could see what she was seeing. Then she gave them her "thumbs up" sign and looked back at the wall again, smiling. Who or what was she seeing? Whatever it was, Anne's experience gave her children a sense of "It's okay".

The next morning the family took their mother back to her peaceful room in the nursing home, filled with flowers and some of her special things. There she drifted in and out of consciousness for the next two days while family and friends spent time with her. Again, one of NurseLink Foundation's beautiful Nepalese "angels" was present in the vigil overnight to give the family and friends a break. These nurses from Nepal were in South Australia to receive our brand of nursing training and qualifications. To me, they already had gifts of genuine caring and the skills required to be a qualified palliative care assistant. I feel the west has much to learn from the east in these exchanges of education.

Back to the story of David and Anne. All the children were present at the time of their mother's death and expressed their appreciation of the added support that NurseLink Foundation was able to bring to the bedside. It was indeed "hospice in place," which could well be a cost-effective model of care for the future. I like to believe it was the devotion of Anne and David that beckoned, in some form, on the blank wall in the hospital emergency department and which attracted Anne's attention.

REFERENCES & INFLUENCES

Alexander, Eben. (2013) *Proof of Heaven*, Simon and Schuster, New York

Chodron, Pema. (1991) *The Wisdom of No Escape and a Path to Loving Kindness,* Shambhala Publications, USA

Calabria, Michael D. and Macrae, Janet A. (1994) *Suggestions for Thought by Florence Nightingale – Selections and Commentaries,* University of Pennsylvania Press, USA

Dossey, Larry. (1993) *Healing Words* – The Power of prayer and the practice of medicine, HarperCollins Publishers, New York

Griffiths, Bede. (1982) *The Marriage of East and West,* William Collins, London

Holecek, Andrew. (2013) *Preparing to Die – Practical Advice and Spiritual Wisdom from the Tibetan Buddhist Tradition,* Shambhala Publications, USA

Harvey, Andrew. (2006) *A Walk with Four Spiritual Guides,* SkyLight, USA

Macrae, Janet. (1988) *Therapeutic Touch* – A practical guide, Alfred A Knopf Inc, New York

Mindell, Amy. (1999) *Coma: A Healing Journey* – A guide for family, friends and helpers, Lao Tse Press, Portland, Oregon

Moore, Thomas. (2010) *Care of the Soul in Medicine* – Hay House, Inc.: www.hayhouse.com

Myss, Caroline. (2007) *Entering the Castle – An inner path to God and your soul,* Simon & Schuster, New York

Nugent, Joy. (2009) *New Nursing,* NurseLink Foundation, Adelaide SA www.joynugent.com

Rinpoche, Sogyal. (1992) *The Tibetan Book of Living and Dying,* Random House, UK Ltd

Tacey, David. (2003) *The Spirituality Revolution – the emergence of contemporary spirituality,* HarperCollins Publishers, Australia

The Age Health and Care Study Group (UK) (1999). *The Future of Health and Care of Older People,* cited in Barbato, M (2010) *Caring for the Living and the Dying,* 2nd ed., Kiama, NSW, p.186

Van Praagh, (2008) *Ghosts Among Us: Uncovering the Truth About the Other Side,* HarperCollins Publishers, USA

Webb, Val. (2002) *Florence Nightingale – The Making of a Radical Theologian,* Chalice Press, USA

Printed in the United States
By Bookmasters